SATAN'S BUSHEL

SATAN'S BUSHEL

BY

GARET GARRETT

AUTHOR OF "THE DRIVER," "THE CINDER BUGGY," ETC.

Auburn, Alabama
The Ludwig von Mises Institute
2007

Reprinted 2007 and 2018 Ludwig von Mises Institute
ISBN: 9781610160896

SATAN'S BUSHEL

CHAPTER I

WHY they asked me to their grayish feast they perhaps did not know themselves. I was a writing person who happened to know their language. They were men of the market place, pillars thereof, with much in common and nothing in friendship. I had been surprised to see them together until I remembered the news that was running in big headlines all over the country.

What inclined them suddenly to one another was the centripetal force of a harrowing experience. They had just appeared at Washington before a Committee of Congress to bear witness for that honorable system of use and sorceries that is founded on gambling in wheat —and the mule of public opinion had kicked them in the face. They never saw the mule. They had only felt it. Also they were aware of seeming ridiculous. And having come with one impulse to the seashore to let the thing blow over, they were beginning to be so bored with themselves that when one of them spoke of what they all were thinking the other three silently groaned.

"What did anybody say that wasn't so?" Moberly demanded to know, evidently for the ninety-ninth time.

"Nothing," said Goran, with weary inattention. "Nothing," he added, gently fingering his little beard. Goran was a corporation lawyer who specialized in Board of Trade practice. His business was to keep wheat gambling free and legal, within the letter of the law. He was supposed also to know the ways of the mule.

"Then what's all the damn fuss about?" Moberly continued. "Why do the newspapers do this?"

He was addressing himself to me, obliquely, as his manner was, and I did not answer. The reason was that I did not hear him, not consciously, although afterward I remembered what he said; for the moment I was absent. There had occurred to me that instant an astonishing probability. I had the premonition that something unreal was about to come true.

"You, I'm asking," said Moberly, in a tone to waken me. "You're in that line of business. Why do the newspapers always put us in wrong? Or don't they know any better?"

"I beg your pardon," I said. "I wasn't listening. I was thinking of a tree."

"A tree!" he said.

"An inhabited tree," I said. "Did you know a tree might be inhabited? Neither did I. I don't know it yet for sure. Nor do I know any better. This tree I am thinking of is at the other side of the world. It has a root that reaches all the way through to the Chicago wheat pit."

He disliked to be mystified. So he turned away with a gesture of irritation and went on talking. The others were perfectly stolid, thinking perhaps, as he thought, that I had proposed an enigma with intent to turn it against them.

That was not the case. Not only was I thinking of a certain tree—a monstrous, haunted vegetable that lived at the edge of an Asian forest and had enslaved two fascinated human beings; I seemed actually to see it again. If I closed my eyes, there it was, like an object imagined in a crystal. That the image associated itself in my mind with the practice of gambling in wheat was a natural fact, requiring only to be explained. That a tree in Asia had, as I said, a living root in the Chicago wheat pit, was a romantic fact, not to be taken literally. But what had suddenly occurred to me was altogether strange.

This was nothing less than the probability that months before, almost in the shadow of the tree, the present moment with all its accidental conjunctions had been foretold. The circumstances were vivid in memory. The woman had drawn me a little aside. She stood with her hands behind her, looking away. The sun was in her face, yet her eyes were wide open, and her voice was that of one asleep. "In a far place," she said, "by the water, you will be alone among many people. . . . Four men will meet you there . . . as if by chance. . . . They will take you to sup with them. . . . Tell them everything and tell no one else until then. . . . Only be sure they are the right men. . . . You will think of a sign. Any sign will do."

I was a solitary person who traveled a great deal and had made many acquaintances in the world. Thus the conditions were easily fulfilled. There are many places by the water where one may be unexpectedly picked up for dinner; and four is not an eerie number. And yet, nothing of that kind had happened to me since —not until this evening. And beyond the fact that of all the men I knew these four were about the last I should have thought it likely to meet by chance in one group, there was also this singular coincidence—that they were all bound to feel a lively interest in the subject. She had said I would think of a sign and that any sign would do. I had already invented one. Moberly would never ask. That was certain. He would sooner sweat with curiosity than call the answer to a riddle. One of the others might, especially Goran; and if one did—no, but if Goran did, if he and no other should say, "What about your tree?"—I would take that as a sign—I who had never believed in signs. Thus I left it on the knees of superstition, knowing what I did and how silly it was, yet with the feeling that by such device I gave the event its freedom and put the consequences beyond me.

Dinner was served on a private balcony overhanging the surf. There was no expectation of pleasure in it. Moberly and Goran sat together. Next was Selkirk, a moody and very lucky young speculator, who incessantly smoked cigarettes through a long shell holder with a kind of Oriental calm and seemed never to see the surface of anything. The fourth was Sylvester, a plumb, tan-fisted man, grain merchant and broker, who represented the Board of Trade in an official way.

Their voices one at a time starting and stopping

abruptly left holes of silence in the air. Then other sounds rushed in. One heard again the toothless mumbling of the sea, the brass of a distant band, squeals, cries, laughter, ballyhoo voices, the dying merry-go-round, all the tinkle and patter of life pursuing its aimless recreations up and down the boardwalk.

What they said did not interest me. I listened distantly. They touched without moving it, almost without knowing they had touched it, the ageless, endless, economic reptile that has now so many names it cannot always remember what guise it presents to view. Yet it is never anything but the simple fact that men cannot trust themselves to divide up one another's things. This of course has been true from immemorial time. Only now, with society so constituted that division in minute complexity is vital, since no one any longer may exist by his own goods and efforts alone, the consequences are cross-shaped and oppressive.

The theory underlying their discourse, not formulated, yet clearly implied, was that people live by suspicious, predatory groups in a series of jungles, each group taking toll of the other according to the other's necessities by a natural law of strife.

And all the time I was thinking of a law less compounded than that—the law of a man who hath taken a woman.

Moberly did most of the talking. He made one think of a grain elevator—a stark sudden shape, two tiny windows very high up, a door with no steps or threshold, all dark inside, everything glazed with a fine, clean dust. In speaking he made the same monotonous sound a grain elevator makes when it is not mysteriously still.

The thing he resembled, that precisely he was—a mechanism of dreadful simplicity for manipulating grain. A third more or less of the entire American wheat crop passed annually through his hands. He bought it and sold it for gain. The gain was not his. All the dividend of his work belonged to the Dearborn Grain Corporation, which was an institution existing by virtue of unlimited bank credit. It had a nervous system ramified through the whole bread-eating world. Moberly was its head. All its functions were his. He wore the title of president. Its body was owned by anonymous capital. He did not care. He served his corporate Pharaoh fanatically. From a runner on the Board of Trade he had come up slowly, irresistibly, until now in his own aspect he was greater than the power of money he represented. Having discovered the principle whereby capital, if you have enough of it, overcomes the odds of chance, and with an unlimited amount of credit supporting him, he had reduced the Chicago Board of Trade to the status of a private principality, like that of Monaco, where everyone gambles but the prince of gamblers, who takes the percentage. Able at any time to buy or sell all the visible grain, he terrified other speculators and so laid the game of speculation itself under tribute to his machine. He made and unmade corners; for months at a time he carried the wheat pit in his pocket. His immunity, so far at least, from all those forms of fixed delusion that bewitch and ruin great speculators was owing to the fact that he was not a speculator. Never had he any personal interest in gains and losses.

This was the state of mystery into which a committee of Congress had been making hostile inquiry. Moberly was a tough-minded witness. He believed in corners, in speculation, in gambling unrestrained. His convictions included the law of the jungle, raw and unequivocal. He did not announce it. But when it was suggested to him as a theory of conduct by the keeper of the invisible mule, namely, the chairman of the committee, he seized upon it, expanded it, applied it, proved it with brutal logic—and proved at the same time that he had never had a social idea in his life.

And here he sat, full of amazed soreness, two bright red patches burning on his cheek bones, his roaring pouches distended, expounding it all over again—to himself. Nobody was attending to what he said until of a sudden he broke into new ground.

"And all the time I was loaded," he said. "Loaded with nitroglycerin. Enough to blow their quill feathers off. They knew it. Two members of that committee knew it, and knew that I knew they knew it. Yet they sat there looking at me like owls pretending to be eagles. I might have been a sack of wheat for all the care they had. And I was loaded. Talk about gambling! I'd hate to take such chances. A man might explode accidentally."

"What was the nitroglycerin?" Selkirk asked. His manner was coolly disbelieving. Moberly eyed him aslant and went on:

"I'm going to tell you. What were they so hot to

prove? What was it? That speculation affects the
price of wheat one way or another to everybody's hurt.
If the price goes up the loaf is pinched. If the price
goes down the farmer's ruined. But there's something
else in the price of wheat. That's politics. And they
never speak of it. That's what they're all interested
in. Politics."

"I don't see any nitro yet," said Selkirk, with the
same air as before.

"No, I know you don't," said Moberly. "It's right
there. It's in what I know about politicians. Last
spring my directors came to me and said we had to
have more general prosperity in the country. You
know who my directors are. No secret about that.
Men of affairs in all directions: railroads, banks, man-
ufacturing, and so on. They said we had to have more
prosperity. The quickest way to get it was to put
grain prices up. Couldn't I see my way clear to do
that? If I could they would stand under with all the
credit I needed. I said I'd see, and I did see. When
conditions were right I began to buy grain—all there
was. Wheat was around eighty cents when we started.
First, I told two members of the Cabinet at Washington what we were going to do, and——"

"Why?" Selkirk asked.

Moberly hesitated, was about to answer, then gave
him a glance of disgust and went on:

"——and they were pleased of course, because that
would keep the farmer quiet. Anyway, they hoped it
would. They told the Administration, and everybody
was pleased. Prosperity is what keeps a political party

in office. Then certain members of Congress, among them the two I speak of on the committee—they got hold of it. That was all right. As party managers they were entitled to know. I didn't care. The more of that the better. I didn't expect them to go and dig a grave to bury their information in. They were free to use it if they knew how. If they happened to buy a little wheat, so much to the good. Every little helps. Well, you know what followed. We put wheat to a dollar twenty-five a bushel, and the effect, as my directors had calculated, was to stimulate business all over the place. In one way we were disappointed. Forty-five cents a bushel added to the price of wheat didn't keep the farmer still. He was stirred up by a crowd of politicians out of office, telling him that if speculation was abolished he could weigh his wheat in gold. And to meet this what does the other crowd—the crowd that's in office—what does it do? It gets us down there before that committee and puts the goat sign on us. We have to wear it. We can't say a damned thing. We are wicked speculators. We have only one virtue and that's a secret. We won't spill what we know. Huh!"

"Were you in danger of ornamenting your testimony with a statement like that?" asked Selkirk ironically.

"What would newspaper editors have done with that?" asked Moberly, ignoring Selkirk and looking at me.

"They certainly would not have missed the moral," I answered.

"Which is what?"

"That the power of such an organization as yours to make prosperity and bless a political party by advancing the price of wheat is also the power to unmake prosperity and break an administration by depressing the price."

"But we would never do that," he said.

"People would be less interested in your intentions than in your power," I said.

"Then you don't believe in speculation?"

"I didn't say that," I replied. "You asked me the question how public opinion would act on what you've been saying. It might have raised their quill feathers off, but there wouldn't have been enough left of your institution to wear a feather on."

He was the only one of the four who had no flexibility of mind, no glimpse of self-seeing, no pleasantry in disagreement. It was not for that I disliked him. I knew no reason why I should dislike him, yet all the more I did. Our chemistries were antagonistic. My last rejoinder froze him solid. It was more adverse really than I had wished it to be. A silence fell upon us and I was thinking how to restore the broken conversation when Goran spoke, saying, "Let's change the subject. What about your tree?"

There was the sign; and I was startled by its clarity.

"It's a long story," I said. "Moreover, it's the same subject still."

"I remember you said it had its roots in the wheat pit—the tree," said Goran, "whatever that means. But tell us."

"It concerns Dreadwind," I said.

The name as I pronounced it produced an electrical effect in all four of them, each reacting as his nature was. Selkirk, in the act of gently tapping his cigarette holder over the ash tray, became perfectly still, with his third finger raised, regarding me fixedly. Sylvester straightened his spine and made a slight sound in his throat. I noticed him particularly. Moberly did not visibly stir; his chair creaked. Goran turned half around in his chair, rested his elbow on the back of it and propped his head on his fist, keeping his eyes on me.

"Concerns him now? In the present time?" he asked. "Have you seen him?"

"And Absalom Weaver, too," I said.

"But Weaver's dead," said Goran.

"That may be. It is as one thinks. I have seen his shadow."

"Anyone else?" asked Goran.

"Yes. The woman."

"Who is that?"

"Weaver's daughter."

"One romance more on this barren earth!" said Goran, glistening. "Tell it simply."

You to whom now I am telling the story would perhaps never have heard of Dreadwind. You would not know what there was about him to make four such minds become taut with interest at the sound of his name. He was a speculator, a wooer of chance, commonly to say a gambler, who shook the sills of the wheat pit and then suddenly disappeared. That would be nothing strange by itself. Many speculators do suddenly vanish from view. It is the rule. Generally they leave some memento, be it only a record in the bankruptcy court or an inexpensive mortuary emblem. Dreadwind left not so much as the print of his foot in the dust of La Salle Street. Still, even that is not unheard of altogether. What made his case unique was that he jilted his star. Surely that never happened in the world before. And such a star!—whimsical, tantalizing, never twice in the same aspect, running all over the heavens, yet true, always true to Dreadwind. No other man could have followed it. He understood it, adored it, obeyed it blindly, and was called eccentric. The word was wrong. It defines an orbit. He had no orbit. His movements were unpredictable. And in full career he quit. Or whether he quit or not, he ceased, dissolved, became utterly extinct.

As he ended, so he began—with no explanations whatever. Not that he purposely created any mystery about himself; but he was a silent, solitary, uncommunicative person, who in all possible ways said it with money and disappointed personal curiosity. It perhaps never occurred to him to tell how or whence he came. One day he appeared. That was in Wall Street. His introduction to his broker was money. He had no other; knew not how to get one, he said. The broker could take it or leave it, as he pleased. He said he should probably trade a great deal and wanted fast service in the execution of his orders.

Well, it isn't every day that a golden goose falls out of the sky into a stockbroker's lap; and when it happens the miracle shall not be stared in the mouth. This stranger, giving no account of himself, was seen at once to be more than a cool and practiced votary. He was rare. His operations were so large, so audacious and so unexpected that after a little while the broker found himself in a serious dilemma. True, his till was overflowing with commissions. That was all very well. But the fathers of the stock market had summoned him to kneel on the carpet and hear out of the book of rules that paragraph which forbids unsafe trading. Then they warned him that unless he controlled the gambling cyclone that dwelt in his office he should be deemed guilty of conduct prejudicial to the welfare of the Stock Exchange and expelled therefrom.

Very gently, very ruefully, the broker brought this difficulty to the notice of his client. Dreadwind was not angry. He had rather the look of a man whose feelings are hurt.

"Limits!" he said to himself. "Limits, limits. Is there no game in the world without a limit?"

"One," said the broker.

"What is it?"

"Wheat."

Dreadwind stood still, struck with an idea.

"I've never gambled in wheat," he said. "I never thought of it."

There was a grain ticker in the office. He walked over to it, gazed at it thoughtfully, ran some of the tape through his fingers.

"This isn't like the stock ticker," he said. "I don't remember ever to have looked at a grain ticker before. On the stock ticker the amounts bought and sold are

printed along with the prices.   Here are prices only.
No amounts.''

"That's all," said the broker.   "The prices only.
Amounts are not recorded.''

"You mean there is no record of the amount of
wheat bought and sold in speculation?"

"That's correct.''

"How much wheat could I buy or sell this minute?"
Dreadwind asked, his eye still upon the grain ticker.

"Any amount.''

"A million bushels?"

"Ten million, fifty million.   Any amount.''

"And all that would show here on the tape would
be the price?"

"Yes," said the broker.

"Thanks," said Dreadwind.   "It's two-thirty.   Balance my account, please, and give me the credit in
cash.''

"What are you going to do?" the broker asked.

"Going to the wheat pit," said Dreadwind.   He
added, "I'll have to see.   I don't believe it.''

"You knew him as well as anyone here," I said to
Moberly.   "He must have crossed you often in the
wheat pit.   What did you make of him?"

"He was ten feet high," said Moberly.   "The only
man I was ever afraid of—in the pit, I mean to say.''

That was handsome from Moberly, for, as we all
knew, Dreadwind had several times upset him in the
open market place.   He had been the only man who
dared single handed to engage Moberly in a wheat-pit
contest; and Moberly without his backing of organized

bank credit—Moberly, that is to say, on his own two legs, would have been no match for this invader who knew no rules, no limits and followed a zigzag star.

"I did not know him," I said, beginning the story. "Not until afterward, as I shall tell you. I had never seen him, had in fact no idea of his personality. Therefore, what arrested my attention at sight, besides certain singularities of circumstance, was the personality itself, with no suggestion of its identity—I mean, no suggestion that he was the missing Dreadwind. All the time you must keep in mind the kind of man he was —I should say is. No rule of probability contains him. To say that he acts upon impulse, without reflection, in a headlong manner, is true only so far as it goes. Many people have that weakness. With him it is not a weakness. It is a principle of conduct. The impulse in his case is not ungovernable. It does not possess him and overthrow his judgment. It is the other way around. He takes possession of the impulse, mounting it as it were the enchanted steed of the Arabian Nights, and rides it to its kingdom of consequences. What lies at the end is always a surprise; if it is something he doesn't care for, no matter. Another steed is waiting. Meaning to do this, living for it, he has no baggage. There is nothing behind him. If he has wealth it is portable. He is at any moment ready. A kind of high vagabond, you see."

"You almost persuade me to be likewise," sighed Goran. He was of Polish blood.

"Very exciting," I said. "That was Dreadwind's torment. He could not come to rest. His craving for excitement was a vast hunger. Yet his outwardness, as you know, his superficial aspect, is a mask of perfect serenity. His physical movements are slow, rather hesitating, or as if retarded. I saw them the first time ——"

"Them?" said Moberly, interrupting.

"Yes," said Goran. "There's a woman. Didn't you get that? Absalom Weaver's girl. Go on."

"—— at the edge of a desert," I continued. "My own errand there was one pertaining to oil. I am not an oil expert. But international oil people are interested obliquely in many collateral things: politics, intrigue, personalities, religion, and what not. Such work is confidential. For that reason I hesitate to mention the place explicitly. No matter. It was such a place as you may see almost anywhere in Southwest Asia—a misspelled name on your map, a journey's interruption, a jagged symbol of eternity sticking out of the sand, the tomb of a race untended, mythical tomb of a prophet commercialized.

"I was arriving. They were leaving. There was much make-believe commotion about getting them off. From this I knew that he was free with his money. So he was. He threw it around, not with any air of vanity, for there was nobody of his own kind to be impressed, but simply because its language was instantly understood and a plentiful utterance of it galvanized the action. I was the only other sign of Western civility on the scene and he never so much as glanced at me, though I stood near by, looking on. He observed the preparations, attended to them, spoke now and then to his guide and interpreter a word or two in the tone of voice that dead and sleeping people are not supposed to hear—and all the time his mind was somewhere else.

"The only present reality he seemed conscious of was the woman. I could not imagine what their relations were. His manner toward her was impersonal, formal, even distant; yet that was not his feeling at all. One could sense beneath the manner an aching contradiction. He was absorbed in her utterly. There is no other way to say it. Whatever it was they were doing, or about to do, concerned her; and she herself, not what they did, was his concern.

"And the woman! A more oblivious human being could not be described. What she was concerned with lay far, far away, or it was something that had never been found, possibly something that did not exist. One would have thought she moved in a trance. She saw nothing, said nothing, heard nothing. Even when her camel got to its feet—a disagreeable sensation that one could see was new to her body—even then her face expressed no awareness of the senses. It might have been a camel of her dreams.

"So they went—the stare-blind woman first, the man next, followed by guides and servants, into the rising sun. Ahead of them, on the horizon, many miles away, rose a glinting pyramidal form. In the middle distance was the faint perception of a ruined temple they should pass, some broken stone columns and the torso of a monumental stone figure seated.

"It left a vivid picture with me. What the picture

signified was quest. I made some inquiries about them.
All that anybody knew was that they had come and
gone, no whence or whither. More was suspected. A
very old Arab, thinking perhaps that I should feel
some responsibility for a fellow countryman, con-
fronted me repeatedly with accusing gestures. One
hand was full of gold which he showed; with the other
hand he tapped his forehead and pointed in the direction they had gone.

"The second time was stranger still. I thought it
was. This occurred three months later in Mongolia,
north of the Wall, in a country where you meet your
kind only once or twice a day, and then not without a
sense of personal anxiety. We passed and they did not
see me. That was all. They were mounted on shaggy
little horses, pads for saddles, hair-rope bridles, two
servants following. She was looking straight ahead.
He was still absorbed in her.

"Then the third time was at Buenos Ayres. They
came one evening to the gayest hotel, with no luggage
or servants, looking desperately weary and travel sore,
lodged for the night, and sailed the next morning. I
looked at the registration. The name was Jones—A.
Jones and wife. I was sure that was not the man's
right name. It couldn't be."

"Put in something about the woman. I want to see
her," said Goran.

"I've tried," I said.

"Yes, but something about her appearance," he insisted. "What was her type?"

"I can't describe her," I said. "Not directly in

terms of herself. I never saw her that way. She reminds me of something symbolic."

"What?" Goran asked.

"There's a picture of the virgins descending stone steps. Their feet are bare. They are clad all alike in draperies of classic simplicity, drawn in a little with a girdle just under the arms, giving them a sweet, long-limbed appearance. In their faces there is knowledge without experience—knowledge of existence, none of life. She is that first one with the bent knee thrusting against her drape."

"Now I see her," said Goran. "It's what I thought. Go on."

"A long time later, a year and a half perhaps, I was on my way up the Irawadi River. Business pertaining to oil still. A young Britisher with whom I keep a vow of friendship was then commissioner of one of the Northern Burmese provinces, newly appointed; and I went out of my path to see him. We had resolved the nature of matter and whether man was risen from a low estate or fallen from a high one, when of a sudden he thought to say:

" 'One of your mad Americans has broken loose in my province. That's what you say, isn't it? He's told the British Empire what it cannot do. I'm trying to keep it from becoming a diplomatic incident.' "

" 'Where?' I asked.

" 'Up the river.'

" 'Who is he?'

" 'That's another thing,' he said. 'Whether he's going by an alias or has a false passport I can't make

out. He says his name is Jones—something Jones—
A. Jones, I think. But I have reason to suppose his
real name is—ah—Dread something—yes, Dreadwind. Why do you look so taken up? Do you know
him?'

"I told him of a man named Dreadwind, a Chicago
wheat speculator, who had become suddenly nonexistent; also of the pair I had seen wandering about the
world in a hypnotized condition, and that the name
under which they passed through Buenos Ayres was
A. Jones.

" 'Quite,' he said. 'I'm sure of it. A romance,
clearly. I hate to interfere, and yet ——'

" 'What's the row about?' I asked.

" 'Perfectly silly!' he said. 'It's about an old teak
tree.'

" 'Why make a fuss about one teak tree more or
less?' I asked. 'You've millions of them.'

" 'Now, you see,' he said, 'it isn't so simple quite.
The teak in these forests is controlled by the state and
scientifically cultivated. It has to be cut with reference
to age, condition and new growth. A certain bit of it
is due to be cut. The order goes out. Then it appears
that this particular bit includes one tree for which your
fellow countryman has conceived some sort of wild
infatuation. I don't know what or why. He won't
say. But he says—*he* says—that tree shall not be cut.
The British Empire says it shall be. There you are.'

" 'What will happen?' I asked.

" 'It will be cut.'

" 'Teak wood is a commercial substance,' I said.

'Isn't it a matter money will settle? He probably has plenty of that.'

" 'Yes, he seems to have a lot of money,' the commissioner said, rather acidly. 'He's offered to buy the whole forest. That was silly, wasn't it? Then he corrupted the native officials. Bribed them to spare the tree. That's a very serious offense. The next thing was that he got some kind of magic or witchcraft to be practiced on the tree until now I understand the whole place is weird with superstition about it.'

"The English understand human idiosyncrasy, envy it secretly, and are yet quite capable of dealing in an unromantic manner with its troublesome manifestations. This was altogether true of my friend, the commissioner. He was greatly annoyed; it seemed to him his government had been made to appear ludicrous. It could not cut down a teak tree in its own forest because an American preferred to have it stand. Well, we put the subject aside, thinking of it still, and talked absently of other matters. As we parted he said: 'You're going that way. Perhaps you'll have a look at this tree-fey person.' And he gave me exact directions.

"My curiosity by this time was absurdly moved, and I pursued it in a straight line—as straight as the native means of transportation permitted. On the way, with nothing else to think about, I discovered in myself a sentiment of irrational sympathy for the man; for both of them in fact, but for the man especially. That is the sort of thing I have learned to call a human chemistry. We seem to have nothing to do with it.

Do you know that impulse to serve or befriend in a romantic spirit someone who apparently does not need you at all, a stranger perhaps, one you have never seen before and may never see again?   That is what I mean.   Then again people who do need you, who have rightful claims upon your goods and interest, and whose claims you honor, do not move your sympathies at all.   I'm trying to explain the fact that the mere thought of being able to assist Dreadwind, or Jones, to save his tree gave me a sense of charity, gratitude and pleasure mingled.

"I had been through this country before.   The river and its affluents at the time of year it was are littered with small craft.   I was only surprised that as we neared my destination the number of them seemed to increase.   Presently there was no doubt of it.   More than I had ever seen before at one time so far north were moored at the landing place.   The village was a short distance inland.   A procession was headed that way.   Knowing it to be a small village of bamboo houses with no metropolitan attractions I began to inquire.   A religious ceremony was taking place.   One of a most unusual character.   Then I remembered what the commissioner had said and was not unprepared to hear that the ceremony connected itself with a tree.

"A word about teakwood.   It is in many respects the finest wood there is—dark, heavy, oily, does not crack, warp or shrink, much used in fine shipbuilding and for ornamental carving.   The teak tree grows in isolated, defensive clusters among other trees of the forest, aloof and lordly, sometimes attaining to a height of a hundred and fifty feet, with a girth of twenty-five. But the particular teak tree that had become so suddenly an object of preposterous interest was not one of a cluster. It stood alone at the edge of the forest, sole survivor of its group, for it was of enormous age, much older than anything organic or human in the village near by.

"It was not then, however, that I got my impression of the tree. There was too much going on. In the act of comprehending the scene itself I grasped the fact that here was something new in Asia. The imagination, the cynical daring, the gold, of a Chicago wheat speculator acting through a corrupt, cunning and greedy priestcraft upon native Oriental superstition! Can you imagine it?

"In a ring around the tree stood ten elephants, ornately decorated, their heads pointing in. The most gorgeously geared one bore on its back a miniature temple with an idol indwelling. Next within the elephant circle was a ring of holy devotees in propitiating attitudes. Inside this kneeling circle were the officiating magicians, all in loin cloths. One crawled on all fours around the tree, pretending to be an animal. One was preoccupied with self-torturing gymnastics. One ate a nauseous substance from a dish and spewed it out. Others resting from their grotesque exertions lay prone as if in prayer. A rude clay image suggestively mutilated was an object of grimacing attention. Around the body of the tree was wound some red stuff of hateful texture. Above this, attached to the bark, was the effigy of a gigantic butterfly; and over that a great leering mask. Four men squatting in a square drew snaky, unmusical notes from reed pipes. There was no other sound. Incense was burning at the base of the tree. The pungent odor of it seemed to float through other smells—the smell of elephants, the smell of people, the smell of Eastern food—without touching or mingling. The spectators numbered several thousand, and they had been bought without knowing it. When their eyes should be sated with the spectacle of the tree rite there would be a feast in the village. It was then preparing; and the scent of it, savory to these thin nostrils, was causing the stomach to assert its claims against those of the fascinated soul.

"I turned away in disgust, ashamed of mankind in the sight of trees and noble beasts. It is sickening enough to witness the soul's groveling under fears of the mind's invention when its puerile acts are spontaneous and emotionally true; but here was pretence at the source. The priesthood was bought. Only the people were deceived. At the same time one was obliged to admire Dreadwind's shrewdness. He was creating an enormous superstition—that is to say, a native public opinion, in defense of the tree. The published purpose of all this magic was to cajole, propitiate, persuade to beneficence, a spirit—a western spirit and therefore a hostile one—that had come to dwell in the tree. It followed without saying that the dwelling must not be destroyed, for if it were, then of course the angry spirit would burst forth in the form of a blue bull and take its revenge upon the whole community.

"No figure in the resemblance of Dreadwind was visible among the spectators. As the grand impresario he had a reserved seat and was himself unseen. His dwelling place was a double bamboo house not more than two hundred yards from the tree. From two facts about it—one that it was new and the other that the natives avoided it in a curious way—I guessed it was his.

"He must have observed my approach, for he was at the door when I reached it and admitted me silently, with no mark of surprise.

" 'Why do you do it?' I asked, that sense of disgust controlling my tongue.

"Without answering or reacting in any way whatever to my question he stood looking out through the blind, holding two slats a little apart for that purpose, with his back to me, as if I had been a common interruption. He was in slippers, stockings, riding breeches, wore a loose cotton shirt with a purple silk robe over all, and had a turban thing wound around his head.

"He was very tall. His hair was light yellow, almost white; his eyes were blue, expressing a kind of impersonal wonder; the nose was large and indefinite; the lower part of the face was heavy, denoting sensuality tempered by extreme sensitiveness.

"The interior of the house was rather dim; all the blinds were closed. I made out a table on bamboo legs, fast to the floor; also some bent-wood chairs and an iron cot. The chairs and cot were not of native origin. I wondered how he had got them here. There was nothing else but some grass mats on the floor.

"He turned presently, passed me, sat down by the table and crossed his legs heavily.

" 'What did you say?' he asked.

" 'I said, why do you do this? It's abominable.'

" 'It can't hurt the tree,' he said absently. 'Not even if it were so,' he added. This was like an observation, or a comment, upon his own thoughts, which I was permitted to hear.

" 'If what were so?' I asked.

"Then for the first time he looked at me with a touch of personal interest.

" 'I thought you were an Englishman from the provincial government office,' he said, as if that were somehow explanatory.

" 'You are the most incurious person I ever met,' I said. 'I might be a product of that magic outside for any probability I naturally have in relation to you; and yet you do not ask who or what I am.'

" 'Why should I have to ask?' he said.

"At that I suddenly realized what a meddling, turbid ass I looked. I began to apologize and to account for myself, and became extremely uncomfortable, because even to me what I said sounded as if I were making it up. And that it was true did not save me in the least. My interest and interference alike were gratuitous. He did not encourage me to go on; neither did he offer to stop me. He listened and showed no emotion. I told him under what conditions I had passed him three times in the world, how I had got his name—the name of Jones—from his hotel registration at Buenos Ayres, and how his whereabouts and identity had been re-

vealed to me in a fortuitous manner by my friend the
provincial commissioner, who was exceedingly annoyed
and obliged me to hear what a countryman of mine
was doing in his provincial forest.

"'As for my being Dreadwind,' he said, when I
had finished, 'there's no secret about it. I've used another name for personal convenience, to avoid curiosity
in places where my own name might be known. I am
not hiding. You may tell your friend, the Mister Commissioner, that I have also a passport in my legal name,
if that's what he's worried about.'

"'It isn't,' I said.

" He made no reply to that.

" 'It's his precious teakwood,' I said.

"And he made no reply to that, either.

" 'You're at an impasse with him,' I said. 'He can't
understand why you should be permitted to cross the
British Empire in the management of its own teak in
its own forest, and his official mind is extremely vexed.'

"No answer.

" 'He says the tree will be cut,' I said.

"The rite apparently had been concluded. The ser-
pentine notes of the reed pipes had now a kind of
rhythm, coming nearer, and there was a sense of heavy
bodies stirring. The elephants were passing the house.
Dreadwind got up to look out again.

" 'It won't be cut,' he said, returning.

" 'It's my own blundering fault,' I said, 'that I can't
make you see or feel why I have thrust myself into
this thing.'

" 'Why?' he asked.

"There I hung for a minute.

" 'I don't know why,' I said. 'I may have thought I did. Now that you ask me, I don't. No matter why. Say it pleases me to give you the right to command my friendly offices. There is something to be done, if only we can think of it, and I am anxious to do it.'

" 'I know,' he said very simply, putting forth his hand. 'But there is nothing to be done.'

" 'I've told you the commissioner is an old friend of mine. I've told you also that he is obstinately minded to cut down your tree.'

" 'He won't, though,' said Dreadwind.

" 'But,' I said, 'you can't just sit here with your finger in the lion's eye. There would never be any peace. You don't want to keep up this ghastly mummery outside.'

" 'It's distasteful,' he said. 'I couldn't think of anything else, and it works.'

" 'If there was a reason,' I said suggestively. 'Almost any sort of reason. The commissioner is not official to the core. I know him very well.'

" 'There isn't,' said Dreadwind, and that was final. No further that way.

"I went away knowing just as much as when I came, but with the resolve——"

"You didn't see the woman?" Goran asked.

"Not that time. I saw not the faintest trace of her. I've told you it was a double house, a kind of twin affair. I was in one part of it only——but with the resolve, as I was saying, to pry one teak tree loose from

the British Empire. I had no case. The use of friendship is that in a pinch it needs none.

"'All right,' said the commissioner. 'Show me a
way out.'

"That was easy enough, once the mind were inclined.
Teakwood was an article of commerce. If an American wished to buy a certain quantity more or less and
would agree to cut and deliver it to himself, when, if
and as he wanted it, subject to all the local uses and
customs, and, furthermore, if he agreed to take it all
from a certain forest area to be indicated by metes and
bounds—why, what if that area contained only one
tree? and what if he never took it at all? There was
really no obstacle. The cutting or not cutting of that
particular tree was of no interest to the department of
forests, because it stood all alone.

"'Quite!' said the commissioner. 'You do know
how to beat the government.'

"The next morning a sheaf of papers went up the
river—the teakwood contract in duplicate, long but
lucid; an official covering note from the commissioner
to Mr. Dreadwind, and a personal note from me telling him what it was all about. And with that done I
went the way of my own business.

"I heard from the commissioner that the contract
had been returned to him, duly signed, and nothing
more until one day on my return journey a messenger
found me with a note from Dreadwind asking me to
visit him.

"He came to the river bank to greet me.

"'Be a little careful,' he said as we turned into the

path. 'I find that nothing happens if you give everybody plenty of room. There's a——'

"As he spoke it was there, standing in the path,
barring our way—a cobra on its dignity. We stopped
of course. I waited to see what he would do. He was
in no haste to do anything. For some time he looked
at it steadily; then he began to talk to it, in a coaxing,
conversational tone, half in earnest, half in jest. I
don't remember what he said. He seemed to choose
the words for the sound they made. Presently the
snake dipped its head and glided to one side. We
passed.

" 'You seem to have a way with them,' I remarked.

" 'I hadn't at first,' he said. 'One learns.'

"As we emerged in the clearing where the village
stood I exclaimed, 'How tranquil!'

" 'By contrast, you mean,' he said. 'Yes, thanks to
you.'

" 'What is the state of native superstition now?'
I asked.

" 'Indifferent,' he answered. 'I got the magicians to
undo their work. They banished the spirit, shooed it
away. The tree now is believed to be uninhabited.'

"We were walking toward it. Several times he
took in his breath to speak and then said nothing.
When we were close to the tree he turned, and I
turned, and we stood with our backs to the sun. It
was evening. The shadow of the tree lay before us,
creeping as we watched it. How we came to be watching it I don't quite know. I must have got the suggestion from him. One naturally looks to see what it is

another person has fixed his attention upon; and he was observing the shadow with an air of timed expectation, as if something were about to happen.

" 'There's an Eastern saying that the shadow of a thing is its spirit,' he said.

" 'Do you believe it?' I asked, not in earnest.

" 'That isn't the point,' he said.

"We were silent again.

" 'Huh!' I exclaimed.

" 'You see it?' he asked.

" 'Yes. What an improbable accident.'

"All at once the shadow had assumed a human outline—the outline of a man from the waist up, in profile. It was not only very distinct, like a silhouette; it had character. One knew the kind of man it was, or had been, or would be if he had ever existed. He would be a man who leaned forward in his steps, pressed life for an answer, lived for defeat and loved little things.

" 'If you go to the top of the shadow and get the tree against the sun you will not see how it happens,' said Dreadwind.

"I did as he suggested, with an impulse to walk around the shadow instead of through or on it; and it was as he said. The mass of the tree did not forecast the shadow. However, I shouldn't have thought it would, in that case or any other.

"Just then the figure of a woman appeared, walking toward us from the house. I recognized her at once. She came straight up to us and held out her hand to me. There was no introduction.

" 'Mrs. Jones particularly wished you to come,

he said. I noticed that he hesitated slightly at the name.

"She nodded her head slowly to confirm this and then the three of us stood watching the shadow.

" 'It doesn't change,' said Dreadwind.

"I had already noticed that fact. But the time of its phenomenal duration was really very short—not more than five or six minutes, for then the sun went down with a lurch behind the forest. As this occurred and the shadow was extinguished she went close to the tree and touched it lingeringly. It occurred to me that they did this every evening — that they stood together watching the outline come and go and that then invariably she touched the tree in just that way. Their movements had a settled pattern, even that with which he took possession of her and turned her toward the house again.

"She was no longer in that somnambulant condition I have tried to describe. That state had been succeeded by one much more subtly enigmatic. She was alive to the realities of her environment, listened attentively, reacted normally to whatever happened, spoke with direct simplicity—and was like an object seen through an inverted telescope. She was near as a phenomenal fact and at the same time enormously remote to the senses. Not all the time. There were moments, two or three, when she seemed suddenly magnified as if the telescope had been turned around. Her attitude toward Dreadwind was one of implicit believing. It was distinctly not an attitude of seeing. She seemed to have no sense perception of him whatever. Her gaze never lingered upon him in the natural way of women. The fancy occurred to me that he would give the whole world, if he had it, to be touched by her once as I had seen her touch the tree. There was about them an air of living in suspense, of waiting together for an imminent thing that was taking its time.

"There was a frugal dinner of rice and fruit. Conversation withered and died. Our words rattled about the room like seeds in a dry gourd. Such questions as how long they meant to stay, whether they liked it, and what it was they liked, were foreclosed by circumstances. I tried oil and he wasn't interested; then descriptions of the country farther north where I had been and she at once betrayed symptoms of distress. Neither of them seemed in the least to care for the vocal amenities and we fell at length into utter silence. Presently she rose, thanked me for coming, shook hands again with a cool, firm handclasp, and said good night. He excused himself and retired with her, going, as I supposed, to the other part of the house.

"He was uneasy in his mind when he returned, walked about a bit, then sat down and began to smoke, staring at the ceiling.

" 'Mrs. Jones wishes it,' he said. 'Do you mind?'

" 'Whatever it is,' I said.

" 'I think I told you she was particularly anxious that you should come,' he said. 'Just now she surprised me very much by asking me to tell you everything from the beginning—the whole story, I mean, of why we are here and how it came. She was sure you wouldn't mind.'

" 'She knew,' I said.

"He looked at me quickly. 'She knows many things that cannot be learned,' he said.

"With that he began. I shall not try to reproduce his words. He left much to be filled in by the understanding, especially in those passages which dealt intimately with her. He was naturally an inarticulate person. I shall tell it broadly in the third person. If it isn't always clear, interrupt me."

"Move it," said Goran.

"Did the shadow you speak of resemble Weaver?" Sylvester asked: "The girl's father, I mean."

"As it were his own," I said.

"And now Dreadwind is talking?"

"Yes. Only, as I've said, I shall not use his words. I undertake to tell you what he told me; and that was more than he uttered in syllables. The full strangeness of it occurred to me afterward. It occurs to me now—there through an Oriental night, in the land of the White Elephant and sacred python, to hear a man talking of the Chicago wheat pit, the American grain crop, Western Kansas, the Atchison, Topeka and Santa Fe Railroad, all these things leading to a haunted teak tree in the Burmese forest."

CHAPTER II

DREADWIND was born in New York City. When he was thirteen he got a job as door boy in a Wall Street bucket shop, and his widowed mother supposed he had begun a career in banking. What begins in a bucket shop is a career in pure gambling. Pretending to be a broker, the proprietor of a bucket shop is the same as a race-track bookmaker or the keeper of a gambling house. People bet with him on the rise and fall of shares. If they guess wrong he wins their money. If a number of them happen to guess right he absconds. That is why the bucket shop is both immoral and illegal; why also the bucket shop fraternity is beyond the pale in Wall Street. Its members bear a stigma, like people of the underworld; they cannot be received in respectable financial society. They walk in the same thoroughfares; they eat and drink in the same restaurants. The unsophisticated eye is unable to see wherein they differ from respectability itself. Some of them are very likable to know, yet one shall not know them—that is, not without besmirching oneself with the stigma that is theirs.

There Dreadwind started. At fourteen, because he was tall and alert, he was put to the blackboard, marking up prices for the bettors to see, just as the names of horses and the betting odds against them are chalked up in a pool room. At fifteen he began to bet for him-

self. After seventeen he lived by gambling. He knew
nothing about stocks beyond the names of them; but
his flair for guessing their fluctuations was uncanny
and filled his elders with anguished amazement. After
a while the keepers of that bucket shop declined to take
his bets. Then he went to another. His mother supposed he was advancing, as well she might, since never
before in her life had she known what it was like to
have plenty of money. A year later she died in great
comfort.

Dreadwind was twenty-seven when one day he took
all of his gains in cash and crossed the line into the
rectified air of Wall Street's upper world. He did this
simply for the reason that he had exhausted the possibilities of the other. One after another the bucket-
shop keepers declined to take his bets, because of his
consistent winning, until at last the biggest one flourishing at that time had consented to let him go on only
provided he would confine himself to certain stocks and
keep within certain limits of play. "I'll go where there
are no limits," he said. And that day he appeared in
the office of a Stock Exchange broker, asking to open
a speculative account. And of course, his origin being
what it was, nobody knew him there. The sequel to
that episode we already know. In a very short time
he encountered limits on the Stock Exchange. So
again he took all his wealth in cash and departed for
the Chicago wheat pit, where there were no limits,
leastwise none that had ever been discovered.

In all his life up to that time he had never been west
of the North River, never had been thirty miles outside

of New York City. He had noticed vegetation in the parks and sometimes in suburban gardens. Agriculture was a word that had a pharmaceutical sound; wheat was the raw stuff of bread and rolls, and a farm, to judge from the way people spoke of having been born there, was a romantic place to come from. On the way to Chicago from New York he appears to have been so engrossed in the study of wheat-pit dynamics that for all he saw out-of-doors he might as well have been riding in a subway train. He studied wheat, as he had studied stocks, purely from the point of view of fluctuations. That was a sound way for his purpose. You do not gamble or speculate in things, but in the prices of things.

He gambled in wheat quotations as he had gambled in stock quotations, knowing only concerning the thing itself that it was a vegetable substance called grain, and never thinking of that. All that interested him was the symbol of it, the word wheat, against which were other symbols—that is to say, simple Arabic numerals expressing changes of price.

This is very strange if you do not take it for granted —that a man may buy and sell millions of bushels of wheat with not the remotest interest in the wheat itself, as a food, as a vital commodity, as a sign of civilization. His sole idea of it is a word on the dial that hangs over the wheat pit with a hand spinning round to indicate the alterations of value. Dreadwind knew of course the statistics of wheat. He knew also every detail of the mechanism of wheat speculation. Knowledge of that character is easily acquired. Many have it who never gamble or speculate in grain prices. What made him notable at once in the wheat pit, marked him out as one to be wary of, was the faculty we know and cannot define, an instinct perhaps, or in its lowest term a lucky way with the secrets of futurity. He was not infallible. He made heavy losses; yet in the average, which is all that counts, he did almost from the time of his advent in the wheat pit out-trade, outguess, outreach, the hardest, most glassy-minded crowd of gamblers in the world. Nobody ever knew where or how he stood. His methods were new, daring, pyramidal; they were very dangerous, too, for he seemed always trying to prove to himself that the game was in fact limitless. What might have been the sequel now is needless to imagine. That line of fate was interrupted.

One day he was standing away from the wheat pit, idling his mind, when the trifling incident occurred that changed the course of his life. There was no excitement in the pit; the market was dull. Near Dreadwind a blue-nosed man and a moldy broker were playing checkers. A third man in big glasses with a little gray hat pulled far down in front sauntered up and stood watching the game. The blue-nosed man, without looking up, accosted him lewdly.

"Been up to your farm, ain't you, Joe?"

"Yes," said the man in the little gray hat, his feathers beginning to rise.

"How's rye look?"

"Fine," said the other, biting the word.

In two more moves the blue-nosed man lost the

checker game. Then he rose, stalked across the floor
to the little pit where rye and barley are bought and
sold for future delivery. There he stopped and began
to wave his arms. The man in the little gray hat
turned to Dreadwind.

"Do you see him?—what he's doing?"

"What?"

"He's selling rye. Selling it! You heard him. He
asked me how rye was looking. Rye is looking fine,
I told him. Now he's over there selling it."

"Isn't that the thing to do?" Dreadwind asked.

"That's the very thing to do," came the answer
from under the little gray hat. "That's about all we
do do. I know him. He's off. He's well started. The
price of rye is what? Ninety cents. He won't let it
come up for air, not if he can help it, until it's sixty.
In a few minutes inquiries will be coming in over all the
wires. What's the matter with rye? There's nothing
the matter with rye except I said it was looking fine
and he's over there selling its head off. What will go
out on the wires? What will be printed in every newspaper tomorrow morning? There's a strong bear
movement in rye. The speculative position of rye is
very weak. There's going to be too much rye. There's
no demand for rye. Rye is sick. And what happens?
Thousands of little speculators all over the country
begin to shout sell it—*sell it! sell it!* Six weeks from
now the farmers who produce rye, who plow and sow
and pray and sweat for rye, they will have the real rye
to sell and the price will be sixty cents. The farmer has
got to sell it. He can't afford to wait. Who will buy

it at sixty cents? The same gamblers who are selling it now at ninety cents. And when they are all through the price will go back to what rye is worth—eighty-five, ninety cents again. The farmer has a hell of a chance."

"I don't see yet," said Dreadwind.

"Nobody sees yet," said the little gray hat. "The farmers don't see yet. I don't see yet. What I don't see is what right a man who never worked a day in his life, who produces nothing, who doesn't know whether rye grows on a bush or with the peanuts— what right he has to get up from a game of checkers and sell in five minutes more rye than a hundred farmers can grow in a year?"

"You own a farm?" Dreadwind asked.

"Yes, I own a farm."

"You are a farmer?"

"No, sir. I'm not a farmer. I know better. I own a farm because I like it, and it costs me money."

"What do you call yourself, then?"

"I'm a cash grain dealer. I've been a cash grain dealer for thirty-three years and I say what I damn please about you gamblers."

And as that was all he damn pleased to say just then he pulled his hat farther down in front and walked away.

Dreadwind was astonished. If a member of the Board of Trade could talk in that manner against speculation, and with impunity, then there was much about this institution for him to learn. He looked around him as one may for whom the aspect of familiar things has been suddenly altered, made unfamiliar, by the light of a new idea. The blue-nosed man was still waving his arms, and the price of rye, as Dreadwind could see from where he stood, was already down a cent and a half a bushel. And somewhere farmers were producing the grain that this man was selling. The moldy broker, who had heard it all, got up from the checker board, yawned, stretched and turned toward the wheat pit, looking very bored.

"Who was that man in the gray hat talking to me?" Dreadwind asked him.

"He's one of the lunatics we keep in this asylum," said the broker. " 'J'u'never meet him before? He's over there at the cash tables."

The cash tables. Dreadwind knew there were tables—three rows of marble-topped tables—at one side of the great room. Vaguely he knew also that the men at those tables were grain dealers, not gamblers or speculators. They were buyers and sellers of the grain itself for cash, hence the term, cash tables. But he had never been interested in that function of the grain market; he had never once been on that side of the room where the tables were.

Walking to a point from which he could view the exchange floor as a whole he stood for some time looking at it. The panorama was quite new to him.

On the right were the telegraph and cable stations, each one's premises indicated by an illuminated glass sign as if it were on a public street. He recognized these stations as ganglia from which nerve fibers radiated to every part of the world.

On the left were the cash tables, needing about as much room as the wire stations.

Between them, occupying most of the enormous floor space, were the nits—those hectagonal hollow rostrums with three steps up and three steps down; one for wheat, one for corn, one for oats, one for rye and barley and one for lard and pork.

And how much less man is excited by what he can see and touch than by what he imagines!

From the telegraph and cable stations came the sound of clicking insects swarming. From the cash tables came no audible sound at all. Men moved placidly among them, peering into one-quart sample bags, sniffing the grain, feeling it, judging it, writing down their bargains on little cards, with no fuss or whobub.

But from the pits, out of the bodies of frantic men, came that ceaseless, fluctuating roar so unlike any other system of vibrations audible in the world that natural sounds, even that of the human voice at conversational pitch or the ring of a coin falling on the floor, might be heard through it or in spite of it—every tone in the range of the male voice from falsetto to bass; each tone produced egotistically in strife to be heard; no two tones mingling, for if they did the identity of both would be lost in a chord; no rhythm, no predictable repetition, nothing for the ear to rest upon—a monstrous cacophony to stretch the nerves. The worse the cacophony the more the nerves are stretched and the more they are stretched the worse the sound, until men are a little crazed. And the sound is as absurd as that of the lion, who roars not to frighten the jungle but to move himself. It is unnecessary, that is to say, because business in the pit is not transacted vocally. Buying and selling is by signals of the hand. If man were not an animal excited by the sound of his own voice the pit might be as silent as the tomb.

"Voice of the world bargaining for the great primal necessity—food," writes the Board of Trade publicity agent in a lyric moment. But what passes in the pit is a mythical commodity, not food; millions, *billions*, of bushels of grain that have no existence whatever. An imaginary world with an imaginary stomach clamoring for imaginary food.

Dreadwind was thinking. In a week he had gone through the motions of buying and selling ten million bushels of wheat. That wheat had no reality. The whole ten million bushels would not fill a pint measure. It could go into one's eye and not be felt. There was in all that buying and selling only the idea of wheat. Simply, he had been gambling in the price of it. Suddenly it occurred to him that he would not know wheat if he saw it. What was it like?

He walked toward the cash tables. Passing from the area of the pits to that of the tables was like changing one's world. What he noticed at first was the difference in men. Here were men who worked in ponderable stuff. Their way was a way with substance; their eyes were quiet, not restless and glittering. There were men who went from the tables to the pit and others who went from the pit to the tables, back and forth like emissaries; but there were men in the pit like Dreadwind who had never any business at the tables and men at the tables who knew not their way to the pit; and these were two distinct worlds. The tops of the tables were crowded with little paper bags, each one containing a certified sample of a carload of grain—wheat, corn, oats, barley, rye, and so on. Dreadwind could not tell one from the other. He read first the labels and then compared the grains. The day's cash business was nearly finished. Most of the samples were abandoned. They were to be swept away. A number of bags had been overturned.

Dreadwind began to touch the grain. Running it through his fingers gave him a voluptuous sensation. He was seized with a longing, a tactile hunger, to plunge his bare arms into a mass of grain, even to bathe in it. But here were only these quart-bags full. He thrust his fingers into them, then poured the grain over his wrists, and the thrill he got from its cool, clean, caressing contact was inexpressible. Its fragrance stirred cells of hidden knowledge.

I am trying to tell you what it was that occurred to him then and there. It was very important. He could not explain it. Neither can I. It was an emotional experience. Knowledge was a word he found after much groping; it seemed to say what he felt.

*   *   *

"I know what he meant," said Moberly. "Grain does that to you."

"Can you describe what it does to you?" I asked.

"No," he answered, meditating. Then he said: "It tells you something—something you already know and can't remember."

We stared at him. He had never been suspected of that kind of feeling about grain—of any feeling about it whatever. And he did know. For that was saying in another way what Dreadwind said.

*   *   *

It was characteristic of Dreadwind that he set out immediately to track wheat to its source. His curiosity, once moved, isolated its object and pursued it with a single eye. Thirty-six hours later he was in Western Kansas, on the Sante Fe Railroad, lying in a Pullman berth with his nose pressed against the window screen. His senses were weary and staggering under a load of new impressions. And he could not sleep. His tentative destination was farther on. It would be reached about breakfast time.

Riding by railway through the wheat fields on a very warm May evening is an exquisite experience if you give yourself to it. All sounds are muted. Those that are naturally harsh become pleasing and satiny. I suppose this is from the fact that the grassy ocean absorbs them, somewhat as snow does. The shriek of the locomotive at road crossings is like an echo. The wheels on the rails sound like a lathe tool cutting soft iron. You would think the train was stealing its

way on tiptoe for fear of waking something. And all
the time the air is vibrant and musical with the rhythm
of phantom castanets playing just on and under the
lowest pitch audible to the human ear. And that aro-
matic pungency of the growing wheat! The smell of
the sea, so fresh and clean, is a fabricated, purified
smell. This is a living untainted essence, originally
sweet—flavor of sunlight trapped in the dew.

The train stopped. All Dreadwind could see of the
place was a cross of light formed on the wire screen
of the car window by a country street lamp in the distance. A medley of voices spread suddenly on the
night air—hotel bus drivers calling for fares, trainmen
and station agents disputing in haste, a woman insisting on what was wrong with corporate management—
and above all that vocal commotion in the human pond
could be heard the scolding of frogs and the titter of
crickets.

Of a sudden Dreadwind decided to alight at this
place. He astonished the porter by appearing on the
car platform with his bag in one hand, his collar and
tie in the other, just as the train was starting. A moment later he stood on the cinders watching the red and
green tail lights of the train disappear down the right
of way. Then he tied his shoes, put on his collar, and
looked around. He had been in the last coach. The
station was a hundred yards away. He turned his
head and when he looked again the station had vanished. The lights were out. A motor of the waggle-
tail species made the familiar sound of a buzz saw
tearing its way through a knot and coming suddenly

into soft stuff. After that a cool stillness descended upon the place, pierced by the hum of the telegraph wires and the hymn of insect life.

Dreadwind was alone in the country for the first time in his life.

He walked toward the station; its mass came into outline through the darkness. A voice within responded to his knock. What did he want?

"Where is the town?" he asked.

"Up the road about a mile," said the voice.

There seemed but one way. It was the way the motor had gone. But that was the wrong way, and presently Dreadwind was walking on a smooth dirt road that wound its way through the wheat like a path in a dark green sea, gently, ceaselessly rippling.

That dulcet agitation of the air was now a vast, multitudinous harmony. It is so nearly inaudible that if one strains the sense of hearing it is lost; when the sense is relaxed then it may be heard again. There is a faint bass drone, never changing, never ceasing; over that, sometimes very distinct, is a shrill antiphonal effect, swelling and falling in two beats. In and out play the little melodies. Some of them you can hear clearly; others perhaps you only imagine because they ought to be there to complete the symmetry. You cannot hear the rush of the world through space because mercifully that sound is so pitched that it cannot register in our ears. But it is there. You know it is there; and you can somewhat imagine it. And below the range of human hearing is another world of sound, wonderfully orchestrated; here and there musical frag-

ments break faintly through.   And more of this ma-
jestic, submerged composition is audible on a May
night amid the adolescent wheat than at any other
time or place on earth.

You must remember that all of this was to Dreadwind a new and mystical experience. He had the advantage of touching it for the first time as one whose
sensibilities and imagination are fully developed. One
whose acquaintance with nature begins in childhood
may never feel this total wonder. Too much of it
is already familiar before the curiosity of intellect is
added to that of the senses.

"Wheat!" he was saying to himself; "Wheat!" as
if it were a new word, one that he had never pronounced before. There flashed upon his mind a picture of the wheat pit; he remembered its smell and
sound and atmosphere; and turning again to the wheat
he felt—here I use his word—he felt there was something he must acknowledge. What it was he did not
know. But it would be abject—that again is his word
—some form of abject acknowledgment.

In that very instant he was startled by a whispering
that arose everywhere at once, grew louder, came
swiftly nearer, and became suddenly a prolonged hiss.
It ceased as abruptly as it began. A little gust of night
wind had swept the wheat. He knew this. He saw
the wheat running in the wind, saw it change color with
the play of the starlight upon the lighter underside
of its green attire. Nevertheless he was shaken down
to his toes. Knowing what it was did not cancel the
emotion. It occurred again a few minutes later and

again it shook him. He did not care to hear it a third time and so changed his mind about walking the night out. Instead he turned back and found the town.

The next morning at breakfast he asked if there was a grain elevator in the vicinity. There were three. He went to the nearest one. A load of wheat was standing on the scale and three men were disputing about it. One was a farmer, whose grain it was. He was on the wagon seat, slantwise, holding the reins loosely and turned his gaze slowly between the other two. The grain buyer stood in the high doorway, half his length showing above the wagon. He wore a round felt hat and was covered with the fine gray glaze that comes from contact with grain. It is not the impalpable powder that marks a miller and makes him pale. It is less opaque, lies over color transparently like a bloom, and gives the skin a kind of sheen.

The third man was a figure. He could see into the wagon from the ground. He stood on one foot; the other rested on the wheel hub. His hands were knit and the bent left arm lay on the high edge of the wagon box. His aspect was mainly sardonic. The day was very warm; yet he wore coat, waistcoat, collar and tie; a muffler hung loosely about his neck, the ends dangling. His age was perhaps sixty.

He and the grain buyer were looking at each other steadily. The grain buyer was angry. A red glow showed through the glaze on his cheek bones. The old man was ironically suave.

"No. 2," said the grain buyer doggedly.

"No. 1," said the old man. "Now we've said it three times."

They were disputing about the grade of the grain in the wagon, whether it should be called No. 1 or No. 2.

"Take it away yonder," said the grain buyer.

"Yonder's a place you're not thinking of," said the old man. "We're going to sell it here. It isn't as if you were full and didn't want any wheat. You've offered to buy it for No. 2, which means you want it if you can undergrade it."

" 'Tain't yours anyhow," said the grain buyer, looking at the farmer on the wagon seat, who just then looked away, apparently content to let his protagonist settle it.

"Nor yours," said the old man. "Not till you've bought it as No. 1, and no dockage. You've got a record, young man. A record. Two years ago you were declared incompetent to buy grain. The state board of inspectors suspended you and closed your elevator. You were competent enough. That wasn't it. What you took in as No. 3 at one door went out as No. 2 at the other. Grain improved one grade over night just by association with you. It got educated. This wheat you're looking at is already educated. If you can't see your way clear to buy it as No. 1 we'll drive it all the way over to Hutchinson and report you to the state inspectors. But you will see your way clear. And when you have you will mix this fine No. 1 wheat with a lot of musty No. 3 you've got inside, one bushel to five, and sell the lot for No. 2. . . . I know you."

The grain buyer, leaning over the wagon, plunged his arms into the grain several times in different places; lifting them with the palms of his hands upturned he raised wheat from the bottom and let it fall again in yellow cascades. Bending still farther, with his hands on the edge of the wagon, he brought his nose to the places where the grain had been upheaved and sniffed for odors. Then he stood up and scanned it with his eye, betraying indecision.

"No smut, no burn, no garlic," said the old man. "I see you looking at it. Scripture says if thy right eye offend three, pluck it out. Your left alone would be enough to try the children of men. It would so magnify two grains of oats in a wagonload of wheat as to make a pound per bushel dockage. Get the kettle."

The grain buyer reached inside the door and picked up from the floor his test kettle—a one-quart brass measure attached to a hand-beam scale so graduated that the reading at the point where the sliding weight balances the kettleful of grain is exactly the weight of the wheat per bushel. He filled the kettle to overflowing, cut it exactly level with a gentle, slicing motion of the hand, and held it up to read the weight.

"Sixty-one pounds," said the old man. "One pound over the standard. I know without looking. Now sieve it."

Pretending to be deaf the grain buyer emptied the kettle into the wagon, disappeared inside, stooping to set the kettle down, and reappeared with several sieves in his hands. For a moment he hesitated. Then he cast the sieves into the darkness behind him, and leaned against the door jamb, with his feet crossed, looking bored and disgusted.

"Dump it," he said.

The old man took his foot off the wheel hub and began walking about with his gaze on the ground, his hands behind him, waiting for the farmer to unload. Once he stopped suddenly and gave Dreadwind a keen looking over. They did not speak.

Unloading the grain was a simple matter. At one end of the scale platform a trapdoor lifted. The other end of the scale platform began to rise, wagon and all, and the rear end of the wagon having been opened, the grain flowed into the unloading pit and was gone. It took only a minute altogether. The farmer went around to the office to be paid. When he returned with the proceeds in his hand he offered some money to the old man. Dreadwind could not see how much. It was probably the difference between what the farmer alone would have got for his wheat as No. 2 and what the old man had bullied the buyer into paying for it as No. 1, and that difference might have been five cents a bushel, or five dollars on the load. The old man declined the money with an indignant gesture.

"I don't do that for money," he said. "Not that."

The farmer was embarrassed. They drove off together, sitting far apart on the wagon seat, with a feeling of strangeness between them.

The grain buyer was still standing in the doorway with his feet crossed.

"A tough customer," said Dreadwind. "Who is he?"

Wearily the grain buyer withdrew his gaze from the sky, measured and comprehended Dreadwind, then stepped inside and slammed the door.

CHAPTER III

DREADWIND walked back to the hotel, revolving in his mind a project and thinking at the same time on what he had seen. Thus was wheat handled. It had taken a farmer with assistance twenty minutes to sell a wagon load of wheat. That was 100 bushels. In the wheat pit the minimum quantity of wheat that can be bought and sold—the gambling unit—is 5000 bushels, and it changes hand by signal in the twinkling of an eye. How different! The difference between real and imaginary wheat. And how strange all this environment was to a wheat gambler!

The hotel was such a structural vanity as has been rising of recent years in the wheat and cattle towns, extra-modern and sure of it down to the brass name-plate for the clerk on duty; nothing newer, handier, smarter, more superfluous, in Kansas City itself—and nobody in the least awed by it. Visitors go about with their eyebrows raised. Native personages, to show how modern they are, lounge about in their shirt sleeves, without collars, put their feet on the velvet upholstery and drop ashes and matches on the imitation oriental carpets.

Dreadwind came back to it by a side street, having missed the main thoroughfare by one block, and entered through a door that obviously gave into the hotel and yet had no sign or legend upon it. Inside was a narrow hall; and halfway down this hall was an opening with two swinging wicker doors, the use of which was to screen the interior. There was nothing over these doors or on them to indicate what might be taking place inside; but by certain familiar sounds Dreadwind very easily guessed. He pushed the doors open and saw what he expected. It was a spacious room filled with chairs in rows. Across one wall was a large blackboard on which a boy chalked up grain quotations received from a telegraph operator at a sounder to one side. At the left were some partitioned spaces, one with a door marked "Office," one with a window marked "Orders" and one with a window marked "Cashier." Over the blackboard in large gilt letters was a sign: "Anthony Jumper—Broker—Member Chicago Grain Exchange—Grain and Stocks."

It was a bucket shop—a gambling place. The windows were all screened. More than twenty customers were present in the chairs, some of them farmers, some evidently important citizens of the community, including the local banker, all a little furtive and trying very consciously to conceal it. Dreadwind was beguiled. A leopard unawares in a fox's den! Approaching the order window he asked:

"How much wheat may one trade in here?"

"All you want," said the young man behind the window. He was high and weary about it.

"How much margin?"

"Cent a bushel," said the young man, affecting to yawn.

Dreadwind wrote on an order pad: "Sell 200M

May wheat," and pushed it through the window together with two one-thousand-dollar bills.

The silly young order clerk had more vanity than common sense. He had never seen an order as large as that. He ought not to have taken it on his own responsibility. But having made a high spit he could not chew dust. All that he did with the shock of surprise, more than to swallow it, was to adjust his nose glasses with an anaemic gesture of slight personal discomfort.

"All right, sir," he said.

Dreadwind sat down. May wheat was 90 cents on the blackboard. In less than two minutes a boy brought him a memorandum reading: "Sold 200M May wheat at 89⅞."

He was astonished. The celerity with which the report was returned proved what he already knew. This was a bucket shop. His order had not actually been executed. This is to say, the wheat had not been sold by telegraph in the wheat pit at Chicago. There was only the pretense of this having been done. All that had happened was that a bet had been entered on the books of the concern—a bet between Anthony Jumper and an unknown client on the price of 200,000 bushels of wheat. But a bet of that size was rather large to be accepted with all coolness in a small-town bucket shop. And Dreadwind was curious to see what would come of it. The price of wheat began to fall. The next quotation made it 89¾, then 89⅝, then 89½.

Presently the wicker doors flew open and shut again.

Mr. Jumper was back from lunch. He was a bald, brisk little man with an ingratiating manner plated upon a metallic surface. First he stopped in the office. A minute later he was with the young man behind the order window to see what business had been doing in his absence. Suddenly he burst forth in a great hurry, crossed the room toward the blackboard, spoke a word to the telegraph operator, and went directly back behind the order window. There he conversed in low tones with the young man, all the time regarding Dreadwind with a shrewd slanting look.

Anyone who knows a bucket shop will understand this pantomime. Jumper saw Dreadwind's transaction in 200,000 bushels of wheat as the young man had entered it on the betting sheet. Then he saw on the blackboard that the price of wheat was falling. The unknown customer was winning. His first act was to tell the telegrapher to stop passing up prices—to sit on them until further notice. That would give him time to think. Having thus postponed disaster he went back behind the window to have a good look at Dreadwind and resolve a course of action. All of this Dreadwind was amusedly aware of; and he was not surprised when Jumper came and sat down beside him.

Jumper had decided to take his dilemma by the horns. His instinct was sound. He knew the kind of person Dreadwind was.

"This is no place for you," he said quietly, in a confidential voice. "We can't handle your business."

"But you have it," said Dreadwind, showing the memorandum on which it was written: "Sold 200M

May wheat at 89⅞." That was binding. With an uncontrollable impulse Jumper reached for the paper. Dreadwind gently drew it back.

"You're a good sport," said Jumper. "I can size a man up. And you're an old hand at this game. I can see that with one eye. You don't want to upset me, do you? This is just a little affair here. I'm only starting for myself. Took over a business I was working for."

"What's the matter with your wire service?" Dreadwind asked. "Your quotations have stopped."

"Honest, now," said Jumper, ignoring the question, "I can't handle your business. The bank roll won't stand it. You know how that is. That boy was all alone there when you came in. He didn't know any better. He's a nice boy. Got an old mother to look after. Now man to man—we understand each other —just man to man, let's call it off."

"I can read the telegraph instrument," said Dreadwind. "I know what the price of wheat is. It's 88½. I hear it. And the last price on the board is 89½."

Jumper gave vent to a startled sinner's oath. "You ain't one of them ringers that goes around busting up little fellows like me? You ain't, are you? No. You ain't. I can see that."

"If you don't let those quotations go up on the board I'll tell everybody what kind of game you are running," said Dreadwind.

Jumper looked around the room with a desperate air, scanning the wide, wide ocean for a bit of friendly wreckage. Then he relaxed, puffing out his breath.

"I'm up the flue if you do," he said. "Up, up. Gone! Busted! All right. Go ahead and see what you get. No, now listen. See here. You are a good sport all the same. I'm not wrong about a man like you. Let me slip you this two thousand and you tear up that piece of paper. Would you take advantage of me when there was only that idiot alone in the shop? And he with an old mother to think about?"

"Well, on one condition," said Dreadwind. "I want you to tell me something."

"I'll tell you anything," said Jumper. "Only first let's get this off my mind."

"Not yet," said Dreadwind. "First, tell me, who is that——"

"Please," pleaded Jumper, "let me slip you this money and tear up that piece of paper."

"I'm asking," said Dreadwind, "who is that totem pole with the owl face in the last chair behind us?"

The person he indicated was the old man who had bullied the grain buyer at the elevator. He entered the room right after Dreadwind and had been regarding him ever since in an overt manner. With Jumper, Dreadwind was not really serious. All the time he meant to take the back money and cancel the bet. But he could not resist the impulse to stretch it a bit; and casting about for some pretext on which to prolong the bucket-shop keeper's agony he thought of the old man, who had evidently followed him from the elevator.

Jumper screwed round in his chair.

"Him? He's nobody," he said. "He comes with

the chinch bugs about this time of year. Never was in
here before. But I'm only starting for myself, as I
told you. I used to see him in the place I was working."

"What's his name?"

"Weaver."

"His first name?"

"Absalom. What about him? He's queer, that's
all."

"What's queer about him?"

"Nothing you can say. Just the way he comes and
goes. All the farmers know him."

"Does he ever trade?"

"Not that I know of. I never saw him trade."

"But you've heard of his trading?"

"I've heard it said he had something once and lost
it trading."

"Where does he live?"

"Not around here. I'm telling you, he comes and
goes. That's all I know. Please let me slip you this
money. It's burning a hole in me."

Dreadwind handed him the slip of paper on which
their bet was recorded and Jumper surreptitiously returned him his two one-thousand-dollar bills.

"Wait a minute," said Jumper. He went again to
the blackboard, not hurriedly this time, and spoke in
a casual manner to the telegrapher. The telegrapher
made no vocal response; but all at once the quotations
began to go up on the board. Jumper returned to
Dreadwind and sat down.

"Now, I don't want you to think I run this place

crooked," he said. "I don't. It's straight. There's
no use trying to fool you. We talk the same language.
What I'm saying is honest. I never stopped the quotations that way before. I wouldn't. But you had me
where I couldn't help myself. You know yourself how
that is."

Dreadwind nodded his head. Jumper went on.

"Of course you do. I'd 'a' gone up the flue in a
minute. No, sir, when I started here I made up my
mind to play it on the level. Why not? They lose
their money anyhow. I couldn't do anything to quotations that would make them lose it any faster. I'm
satisfied. Maybe you're in this line yourself?"

"Not exactly," said Dreadwind.

"I don't quite get you yet," said Jumper. "But I
know the kind of man you are, and you know all about
this game, don't you?"

"Something," said Dreadwind modestly.

"Well, as I see it, it's all right," said Jumper. "As
I say, they will lose their money anyhow. They would
lose it just the same if we sent their orders to Chicago
to be executed regular, like they think we do. The only
difference would be then that them big Chicago gamblers, them Dreadwinds and others, would get it. They
don't need it and we do. When we get it we spend
it here in the town. I've just built a house here.
That's what I mean. Suppose I sent their orders to
the Chicago Board of Trade instead of sticking them
on a spike back of that partition. That money I built
a house with would have gone to Chicago, wouldn't it?
As it is it stays here in the community. That's better.

And what difference does it make to them? Not a bit
of difference. They would lose it anyhow. I've
thought this all out because I'm honest."

"Do farmers trade with you much?" asked Dreadwind.

"They're my best customers."

"And they always lose?"

"That's what I'm telling you. Not the farmers
only. I've never seen a man beat the game yet, not in
the long run. All you have to do is keep on with him
and you get his money. Maybe you can beat it. I
don't know. I think maybe you can. That's why I
was so scared. But the farmers—you were speaking
of them—it's funny. They never do but one thing."

"What's that?"

"Buy, buy, buy. They don't know anything else.
Sometimes I feel like saying to them: 'You make it,
don't you? You grow it, don't you? You take all the
risk to begin with. Then you come in here and buy it
as a gamble.' I don't understand them. If I was a
farmer I'd never do anything but sell, if I gambled at
all, and I wouldn't. But that would be logical, wouldn't
it? I feel like telling them sometimes. But I don't.
What's the use? They'd lose it anyhow."

He sighed for the foibles of mankind. Dreadwind
rose. They shook hands.

"Thanks," said Jumper for the last time. "I was
never wrong about a man yet."

The old man was gone. Dreadwind had not seen
him go, and he was disappointed, for he meant to have
contact with him. He strolled about the streets on the

chance of finding him again; but he had vanished, and casual inquiries were of no avail. "It's a whim only," said Dreadwind, "not worth remembering." Still, he did remember it and kept thinking about it as he proceeded to act on the project that had formed in his mind on leaving the grain elevator.

In the middle of the afternoon you might have seen him on the highway, made out in the rig he had furnished himself with in the town—stout shoes, leggings, khaki trousers, a flannel shirt and soft hat. He carried a stick cut from a wayside hedge and had on his back an army knapsack stenciled U. S. A. People nodded pleasantly as he passed and he nodded back at them and did not know they turned to stare.

This he placed as one of the high moments of his life. I envied him. Fancy seeing the country in that way for the first time—receiving one's impressions of of it originally on a fresh negative, through a lens of full power, with nothing expected, nothing familiar, nothing to be taken for granted.

A breeze was stirring. The wheat was in gentle motion. It seemed always to be running toward him, eagerly, excitedly, expectantly, like a friendly dog on crouched steps with its eyes glad and its ears flat. He wished to pet it, stroke it; he heard himself talking to it. After some groping he found a word for the feeling he experienced at that moment. He was flooded, he said, with a sense of profound wisdom. Profound is mine. He said simply wisdom, but with an accent I cannot reproduce. Twice he turned back to the first great field of wheat. The original thrill was

there. Almost he could not bear to part with it. Mind
you, I'm filling in. A man could not talk that way
about his own emotions. Dreadwind at least could not.
What he said was: "Twice I went back to the first field
of wheat I saw." There he paused in the narrative, sat
for a moment in reverie, and then with a little start
went on.

At each turn or rise in the road he stopped. Once
there was a sudden view of an old house between two
great trees at the far edge of a field of wheat; beyond
the house was a brook, back of that a rise of ground
and then some kind of sky. Nothing unusual perhaps.
It appears to have been such a glimpse as sometimes
frames itself in reality, a bit of perfect natural composition that gives one a mysterious sense of self-projec-
tion. I am saying this. What it reminded him of was
a woodcut of spring in the almanac his mother kept on
a nail in her kitchen cupboard. That woodcut had remained vividly in his mind all these years. Always
when he thought of the country he thought of that. It
had been another world. And here it was, that other
world, in being. He was walking in it.

When the sun was low he asked for supper at a
farm-house, choosing a small one. The farmer, in his
stocking feet, was rocking on the side porch. Having
adjusted his mind to Dreadwind's request he looked
out over the fields instead of turning toward the open
door, and called in a loud voice: "Maw! Here's a man
wants to eat supper with us." A long silence; the
farmer motionless, gazing into his fields. Then a
pinched voice from the kitchen: "There ain't much to

eat. If he will be satisfied with what I can pick up. I
don't know." Dreadwind's satisfaction was pledged.
"Well, it ain't ready yet," said the pinched voice. "Give
him a chair." And whereas until then indoors had
been tomblike, now began suddenly a series of prom-
issory sounds—the rattle of stove lids, a clangor of
pans, a clicking of dishes, and very soon the sizzle of
meat falling into hot fat.

"Wheat looks very good," said Dreadwind at a
hazard.

"Been looking at it myself," said the farmer. "You
can't tell from the road. Sometimes you can't tell until
it's threshed. Wheat you think's fine threshes light.
Wheat you think's spindly and light does better,
though that ain't so often as like the other way."

"The country looks prosperous," said Dreadwind,
after a dead pause.

"Does it?" said the farmer. "Maybe so."

"Isn't it?"

"That's according to how you look at it," said the
farmer, aggressively crossing his knees the other way.

The seam was open. He began to complain. He
complained of the weather, of pests, of a certain man's
luck who thought it was good management, of the price
of farm implements, of the Government for never doing anything, of the trusts that controlled its do-noth-
ingness, and of speculators who got all the profit in
everything. Dreadwind noticed that the barn needed
mending. The windmill, the water trough, the hog
fence, the hen shed, the porch floor sagging under the
rocking chair—they all wanted mending. The only

mending he could see anywhere had been done to the farmer's wool socks. A rusty reaper stood under the apple tree.

"Maybe he wants to wash," the woman called from inside. She appeared in the door holding out a hand basin. "Supper's most ready," she added.

When they sat down to it the farmer asked the Lord's blessing on the food and immediately lost himself in the partaking of it.

Now the woman began. There was no fresh meat. Only ham. Nobody was expected to come in like this at suppertime. The ham was not as good as it ought to be because just as it was ready to come out of the smokehouse her mother's cousin who lived in the next county was seized in the night and they went over to her in haste and were gone three days and the boy didn't know enough to take the meat out. Anyway, they hadn't told him to. But it got smoked too much. If the stranger had come an hour earlier there might have been chicken. If it was Saturday there would be fresh bread. If it was Tuesday there would be fresh butter. And buttermilk. Or maybe he didn't like buttermilk? Some didn't who never knew what it was to get it fresh. The preserves were not sweet enough. Sugar had been so high. The potatoes were old because the new ones were late. She might ask him if he would have some eggs except that there wouldn't be any eggs until tomorrow. The last one had gone to fill out a crate the expressman called for, a day ahead of his regular time, on account of the fact he was going to be married.

No matter. The food was delicious. Ham, cream gravy, fried potatoes, asparagus, buttered beets, pot cheese, chopped pickles, pears in sirup and coconut cake—delicious and plenty, all but the coffee, which was plenty only. When the meal was over Dreadwind wished to pay a dollar. The woman wanted twenty-five cents. The farmer was not interested. He seemed embarrassed at this commercial translation of an act of hospitality, and retired to the rocking-chair on the porch. A quarter it had to be. Dreadwind paid it and took his leave, conscious at the end of some slight con-straint on both sides. The woman shook hands with him as he extended his, but immediately turned her back and began to rattle the dishes. The farmer's good-bye from the rocking-chair was a little bit curt. Dreadwind did not understand it.

In the narrative he lingered over this incident. Whether it was that it touched him in some subtle way he could not explain or that he needed time for what was to come next, I leave you to guess. It was a new world, full of strange people, with shy impulses both toward and away from one. His first experiences with them would be likely to leave a vivid impress. Yet I rather think he dwelt on this episode to gain time. The beginning of the great romance was only a few miles farther on. He was coming to it.

Darkness came, seeming to rise out of the ground, and he was still walking, musing, thinking out loud, wondering a little where he should lodge for the night, or whether to sleep in the open air by the roadside, when he caught a twinkling of lights in the foliage some distance ahead; and there was no sign of a village. As he came nearer he heard a man's voice, rhetorically pitched; and then a scene unfolded. A lawn in front of a farmhouse was dimly lighted by lanterns swung in the trees. Twenty men or more were seated there on chairs and benches, a few on the porch stoop in the background. On a box, under three lanterns on a horizontal stick nailed to a tree, stood the speaker. There were some pamphlets at his feet, some under his left arm, one open in his right hand. His theme was coöperation. He was reading from the literature of the American Farm Bureau Federation, this:

"Coöperative marketing is the golden rule of agriculture. The fever and fear are removed from the season of the harvest. The farmer who is favored by season or seedtime with an early harvet pools his crop with that of his neighbor. For like quality and grade of product they receive the same price. Their crop moves to market from their common bin in orderly fashion. There is no surplus bugaboo chasing relentlessly on their heels and breathing the scorching fire of ruinous prices. Neighbor joins with neighbor. They pool their product. They share and share alike in the new system of economic justice for agriculture. All this is precisely what the Great Teacher meant when he said: 'Therefore, whatsoever ye would that men should do unto you do ye even so unto them.' "

The speaker cast that pamphlet down and opened another. He would deal now with facts. Already coöperative associations were marketing more than a billion dollars' worth of farm produce annually. Take prunes, the perfect example of successful coöperation in marketing. Everybody knew what the prune growers had done. Here, of course, the problem was wheat, and there were those who said that what the prune growers had done wheat growers couldn't because wheat was different—that prunes were prunes and wheat was wheat. He would show them how wrong they were. He would show them there was no difference. He was there to tell them that prunes were wheat and wheat was prunes. He would prove it.

The proof was intricate. Dreadwind's attention wandered from the speaker to the audience. His position was such that he could see the faces and remain himself unseen, leaning on the fence, outside the lighted circle. And there at the far edge of the group, a little apart, sat his old man—namely, Absalom Weaver. He was not alone. Beside him sat a young woman with her two hands in her lap, her eyes fixed on the speaker, her mind apparently in rapt contemplation of the abstract idea that wheat was prunes.

How simple it sounds!

There sat a young woman. But what if she were the only young woman in the world? And when this manner of thing happens she is. The unsearchable moment, I suppose, is that in which the man for the first time sees all women in one, the eternal symbol embodied and undivided, and conceives a fixation for it. No other event in life is comparable to this. Everything that ever occurred in the universe must have occurred precisely as it did through infinite chance to bring it to pass. And there is the choice of only one or two commonplace phrases to describe it. He fell in love with her. Yes? What does that mean?

At this point of the story he groped, wandered into irrelevancies, fell into sudden silences. It seemed like trying to recall a very old dream. He was for going on. I brought him back. What did he do? I wanted to know what he did. He remembered standing behind her, close enough to have touched her; how he got there he could not recall. One will suppose that he opened the gate with his two hands, went in on his two feet, walked around the group and stood near her. No one would have been likely to notice him.

It was curious that he should have remembered something that had nothing to do with it. That was the speaker's climax. It was this:

"The farmer sells and the farmer buys. What does he sell? A primal substance, the food that sustains the world. What does he buy? Machinery, wagons, building materials, hardware, cloth, sugar, sometimes a piano or a phonograph—such things. When he sells the primal substance what does he say to the buyer? He says: 'How much will you give me?' But when he buys what does he say? He says: 'How much will you take?' Think it over. In every case it is like that: 'How much will you give me?' for what he sells: 'How much will you take?' for what he buys."

At this an assenting, brooding murmur went through the crowd. Until then it had listened in a stolid manner. Now the speaker, who was an organizer for a state-wide coöperative marketing association, began to solicit signatures, passing the printed blanks around.

A voice was lifted up, calling, "Weaver!"

The old man did not stir. He sat with his hands clasped around an upraised knee. Other voices took up his name, calling: "Ab! . . . Weaver! . . . Absalom Weaver! What about it?"

Respect and familiarity were mingled in these voices; and as they kept insisting the old man slowly arose.

"Sign," he said. "Go on and sign. It will be educating. Each generation must learn for itself and when it has learned it is ready to die."

With that he sat down. It was not enough. They continued to call upon him. He arose again and said:

"Luke, eighteenth chapter, twenty-second verse: 'Sell all that thou hast and follow me.' That is the sublime thought for coöperative marketing. I commend it to you. It works. But it works in heaven. Don't let anybody tell you it will pay on earth."

And a second time he sat down. Their demand became explicit. They said: "Preach us a sermon." And when it was irresistible he got up and walked to the place under the three lanterns. He did not stand on the box.

Dreadwind remembered distinctly that now he sat down beside the young woman and spoke to her.

"Is that your father?" he asked.

"Yes," she said; and looked at him with surprise. It was clear that she was surprised, not at having been spoken to by a stranger, for as to that she was quite indifferent, but that anyone should have asked that question.

"What is your name?" he asked.

"Cordelia," she answered without looking at him again. Her gaze followed her father. He had not yet begun to speak, but was peering about in the grass, stooping here and there to pluck a bit of vegetation. He walked as far as the fence for a bramble leaf. Returning he snapped a twig from the elm above his head and faced them.

"This natural elm," he began, with an admiring look at the tree, "was once a tiny thing. A sheep might have eaten it at one bite. Every living thing around it was hostile and injurious. And it survived. It grew. It took its profit. It became tall and powerful beyond the reach of enemies. What preserved it—coöperative marketing? What gave it power—a law from Congress? What gave it fullness—the Golden Rule? On what was its strength founded—a fraternal spirit? You know better. Your instincts tell you no. It saved itself. It found its own greatness. How? By fighting. Did you know that plants fight? If only you could see the deadly, ceaseless warfare among plants this lovely landscape would terrify you. It would make you think man's struggles tame. I will show you some glimpses of it.

"I hold up this leaf from the elm. The reason it is flat and thin is that the peaceable work of its life is to gather nourishment for the tree from the air. Therefore it must have as much surface as possible to touch the air with. But it has another work to do. A grisly work. A natural work all the same. It must fight. For that use it is pointed at the end as you see and has

teeth around the edge—these. The first thing the elm
plant does is to grow straight up out of the ground with
a spear thrust, its leaves rolled tightly together. Its
enemies do not notice it. Then suddenly each leaf
spreads itself out and with its teeth attacks other
plants; it overturns them, holds them out of the sunlight, drowns them. And this is the tree! Do you
wonder why the elm plant does not overrun the earth?
Because other plants fight back, each in its own way.
I show you a blade of grass. It has no teeth. How
can it fight? Perhaps it lives by love and sweetness.
It does not. It grows very fast by stealth, taking up so
little room that nothing else minds, until all at once it
is tall and strong enough to throw out blades in every
direction and fall upon other plants. It smothers them
to death. Then the bramble. I care not for the
bramble. Not because it fights. For another reason.
Here is its weapon. Besides the spear point and the
teeth the bramble leaf you see is in five parts, like one's
hand. It is a hand in fact, and one very hard to cast
off. When it cannot overthrow and kill an enemy as
the elm does, it climbs up his back to light and air, and
in fact prefers that opportunity, gaining its profit not
in natural combat but in shrewd advantage, like the
middleman. Another plant I would like to show you.
There is one near by. Unfortunately it would be in-
convenient to exhibit him in these circumstances. His
familiar name is honeysuckle. He is sleek, suave, bril-
liantly arrayed, and you would not suspect his nature,
which is that of the preying speculator. Once you are
in his toils it is hopeless. If you have not drowned

or smothered him at first he will get you. The way of this plant is to twist itself round and round another and strangle it.

"This awful strife is universal in plant life. There are no exemptions. Among animals it is not so fierce. They can run from one another. Plants must fight it out where they stand. They must live or die on the spot. Among plants of one kind there is rivalry. The weak fall out and die; the better survive. That is the principle of natural selection. But all plants of one kind fight alike against plants of all other kinds. That is the law of their strength. None is helped but who first helps himself. A race of plants that had wasted its time waiting for Congress to give it light and air, or for a state bureau with hired agents to organize it by the Golden Rule, or had been persuaded that its interests were in common with those of the consumer, would have disappeared from the earth.

"The farmer is like a plant. He cannot run. He is rooted. He shall live or die on the spot. But there is no plant like a farmer. There are nobles, ruffians, drudges, drones, harlots, speculators, bankers, thieves and scalawags, all these among plants, but no idiots, saying, 'How much will you give?' and 'What will you take?' Until you fight as the elm fights, take as the elm takes, think as the elm thinks, you will never be powerful and cannot be wise."

CHAPTER IV

WEAVER stopped. The state bureau's organizer tried to speak again and got somewhat excited in the futility of the effort. Everybody was up and moving about, with no more attention for him. He did at length impound an audience of four calm and wordless minds unable to say either yes or no or to get away from him. The rest coalesced in groups of two and three, some to depart at once, others to exchange news and information of the countryside. There were cries: "Good night. . . . Wait a minute. . . . Take Ann with you. .. . . We're going too. . . . How's mother?"

Weaver spoke to no one, nor did anyone speak to him. He was as a bishop among them, not to be spoken to unless he wished it; also it was apparent that he troubled their minds. They were eager to hear him and then never knew what to do with what he said. He walked straight from under the three lanterns toward his daughter, looking neither right nor left, but only at her. She rose to meet him. He took her arm and they walked away together. Dreadwind followed them. The moon had come up. One could see clearly in the road. After having followed them at a distance for some time he quickened his steps to overtake them.

"May I walk with you a bit?" he asked, coming beside the girl.

"That ye walk not as other Gentiles," said Weaver. "Walk about Zion, go round about her."

Dreadwind took the hint and came around to the old man's side.

"This is the third time I've seen you today," he said.

"Twice," said the old man sharply. "Twice. Mind what you say."

And Dreadwind took another hint, which was that Weaver wished his appearance in the bucket shop not to be mentioned.

"I heard what you said to them just now," he said— Dreadwind said. "I was particularly interested," he added, "in that part of your parable about the honeysuckle."

"You might be," said Weaver.

This was unexpected and not to be digested in a moment. The pause became awkward and it was left to Dreadwind to end it.

"My name is Dreadwind," he said, unable to think of anything better.

"I know who you are," said the old man.

"And your name is Weaver?" said Dreadwind, rather vacantly.

"Everybody knows that," the old man retorted.

Just then Dreadwind caught a glance from the girl. In it he read, or thought he read, both mild surprise at his pertinacity and a sign not to mind her father's curtness. At any rate, if he needed encouragement, which is doubtful, he was encouraged to go on.

"And that part about the elm tree," he continued.

"The illustration itself was perfectly clear until you seemed to turn it against the idea of coöperation. Do not the leaves of the elm coöperate?"

This was a challenge to the old man's mind and his manner somewhat relented.

"A tree is a community," he said, "a complex society of many different parts, separately acting, all governed by one spirit which we call an instinct. The leaves, do you say, coöperate for the preservation of the whole? That is in seeming only. Each leaf strives with all its might to take care of itself alone, and it is so ordered that the result of this shall be the good of the tree. The leaves themselves know nothing about it. What each leaf does for itself is good for the tree, but no leaf ever stops to think of that. It thinks only of itself. And because all the leaves think alike they appear to coöperate. Call it coöperation if you like. But will you say that elms as elms coöperate? They have no common bin; they do not share and share alike; they have no sick religion of equality. They contend with each other for advantage. What they have in common is an instinct—one way of fighting against all other plants. That is what the farmer needs. If farmers, like elm trees, had a common fighting instinct, then every individual selfishly attending to his own profit would be working for the good of the race without thinking of it and coöperation would be what it is and should be—namely, a natural means and not an end to which you shall need to be exhorted. It would simply occur. What they tell the farmer is that coöperation is a golden end. Ha! What would they

accomplish? Elm would share with elm that all might
be lean alike."

"What would you do?" Dreadwind asked.

"Nothing," Weaver answered. "Do nothing. It
amuses me to torment the place where their minds
ought to be. The farmer has the stomach of the world
in his hands and cannot make it pay. Instead he
drudges for it. He is a slave vegetable without any
brains at all. . . . Good night."

The two turned abruptly out of the road and passed
through a gate. Dreadwind stood alone in the moon-
light, thinking of what you may guess. Certainly not
of coöperative marketing. The girl had looked at him
only that one time and was afterward apparently unaware of his existence.

He was weary from walking. Not a great distance
on he saw a straw stack close by the road and pitched
his bed there; which is to say, he cast himself down in
the straw and fell asleep.

He dreamed a honeysuckle had him by the neck and
smothered him with its flowers; and it was not at all
disagreeable. Very decidedly otherwise, in fact, except that the edges of its leaves were sharp and pricked
his face. There was some baffling circumstance in the
case. It seemed there was a hostile tree that forbade
him to touch the honeysuckle vine, as he longed to do;
and he never knew what might have happened, for he
came awake with a start, as if he had heard voices.
Dawn was breaking. He sat up and looked around,
slowly reconstructing the realities, and heard the voices
again. This time there was no doubt of it. They

were near, just around the straw stack, and coming nearer.

Weaver and Cordelia appeared. Not in the least astonished at the sight of a man sitting on the edge of that kind of bed, they deflected their steps and meant to pass him without speaking. It occurred to Dreadwind to wonder why Weaver, knowing who he was, showed no curiosity about him. For a man to be found sleeping in a straw stack might be common enough; but not a man like himself.

"Good morning," he said, as they were going by.

They stopped. The girl regarded him frankly but did not speak. A shade of annoyance crossed the old man's face. It was no more than a shade. He was apparently in better humor.

"Good enough if it lasts," he said.

"May I walk with you again?" Dreadwind said.

Weaver regarded him thoughtfully and did not reply directly. "I was rough last night," he said. "I was made to think of it afterward. I was chided for it."

Dreadwind glanced at Cordelia. She was looking away.

"We're not walking," Weaver added. "We've come to a wedding."

"At dawn!" said Dreadwind. "A wedding at dawn?"

"Why not a wedding at dawn, sir?" said Weaver. "The time is perfect." He hesitated. "It isn't private. Anyone may come who knows how to see it. If you don't know I'll show you."

Dreadwind rose and went with them. They crossed the road and entered the edge of a wheat field. There Weaver stopped and his hands began slowly to go apart in a gesture of benediction as he contemplated the wimpling wheat in the strained light of early morning. He spoke of it, or to it, in apostrophe. "Oh, lucid wheat!" he said. "Man's friendly nourishment, multiplying to his want, proudly fawning at his feet."

He stood for some time in this attitude with a rapt expression.

"It seems always to be running toward one," said Dreadwind.

"Ha!" exclaimed the old man, looking at him quickly. "You see that?"

"I see it," said Dreadwind, "and yet I do not understand it. I've been thinking it was an illusion."

"I'll tell you why," said Weaver. "Wheat is tame. It does not fight. Man fights the battle for it, and what you see is gratitude."

"I don't quite see yet," said Dreadwind.

"Reflect," said Weaver. "What was wild wheat like? It was a scrawny grass. You would not know it for kin to this. It had to fight. Half its strength went out in strife. Then man made a bargain with it. If it would devote itself to him and multiply with all its strength according to his needs he would guard it from its enemies, fix it in security and peace, give it a private garden for its nuptials. Trusting man it put aside its weapons; and this is now so long ago it has probably forgotten how to fight. What if man's protection failed? Would it not become a scrawny grass again or more likely perish altogether? Its life is in man's keeping. And for the bread that stays him here man relies upon the ceremony we shall witness, so mysterious that no one understands it, so obscure that few have ever seen it."

*   *   *

"I've seen it," said Moberly. "He's right, though. I don't know a dozen men that have. It's the flowering of the wheat."

This wheat pit automaton! He knew. He had seen it. The recollection of it stirred him suddenly. My dislike for him remained constant as a quantity; only now it began to be balanced by another feeling. The others were as much astonished at him as I was. We eased ourselves around. Goran ordered up some refreshments, Selkirk more cigarettes, and I went on with the story.

*   *   *

Weaver's last few words, I resumed, were spoken with divided attention. He had already begun to examine the wheat stalks, one here, another there, taking care not to hurt or trample them.

Dreadwind and the girl waited and watched him; and he was some distance from them when he fell on his knees, verified his discovery through a magnifying glass and called them to come. They also knelt, to bring their vision into the plane of his.

Can you see it? The three of them kneeling before

a wheat stalk there in the dawn?—the male principle in its two aspects, one blindly pursuing, one defending what it could not possess, the maid between them, all kneeling to observe a microscopic drama in the wheat bud, unaware of the greater drama passing in themselves? Or which is greater? There is perhaps no scale to infinity. Less and greater may be tricks of the finite lens.

The old man offered the glass impersonally, holding it out behind him, without taking his eyes from the wheat stalk. Dreadwind made a gesture to mean that Cordelia should look first. At that she took the glass from her father's hand and put it in his. In the act she looked at him, shaking her head. What her eyes said was: "I've seen it many times. You look." She might as well have said it out loud. The old man was oblivious. However, she didn't say it out loud. She said it the other way. And this slight business aside, between themselves, was amazing sweet to Dreadwind. It was a complete episode, miraculous, creative, with structural proportions, and yet more fragile than a cobweb, so that if one dared to challenge it, or to touch it, instantly it turned to nothingness.

Well, the old man never knew which one of them it was looked first, nor that Cordelia knelt there through forty minutes without moving, except to shake her head each time Dreadwind offered her the glass. She knelt there like a saint at vespers, her weight inclined slightly backward, her hands clasped in front of her, regarding the two aspects of the male principle with that eternal knowledge which is pure innocence.

Weaver was talking. On a spikelet of the wheat stem he indicated a small, greenish swelling.

"That is the church," he said. "We are at the door of the conventicle. In a few minutes it will slowly open and three weary cupids will come out on the steps to rest."

He chuckled.

"Why to rest?" Dreadwind asked.

"To rest," the old man repeated. "You will understand when I tell you what is going on inside. At the very bottom of this little swelling lies the egg. The infinite concavity. The devouring mother principle. The egg is not yet the mother. Every mother is first a bride. This bride is very modest. Not shy, only modest. All that she reveals of herself are two lovely plumes, growing tall and straight inside the bud. Around these plumes and growing very much faster are the three cupids I speak of, whom you shall see when their prank is played. Each of these cupids bears aloft an innumerable number of bridegrooms—I don't know how many—all blindfolded. Now there comes a moment—see! it is happening—the sign is when the door comes a little ajar—a moment when the plumes spread out, and the cupids, standing higher than the plumes, hurl the bridegrooms down. They fall upon those spreading plumes. The bridegrooms are the pollen grains—millions and millions of them. And out of all that number the bride will select one. She does not do this at once. There is first a struggle. She requires it. All those bridegrooms must seek her. They must grow down to her. It becomes a terrific drama. They alternately unite to perform prodigious engineering feats in order to reach her and then engage in combat each one for himself. One succeeds. One she receives. The rest? What becomes of those whom she rejects? It does not matter. They are wasted in Nature's own way. It is so. In every piece of life it is so. Millions of surplus bridegrooms are created only to make sure that the bride in her leisure shall be able to choose one. . . . There! . . . See!"

The bud was slowly bursting. What had been at first an ovoid, greenish swelling now was opening into petals at the top; and out from between the petals as they opened came what Weaver called the cupids and what botanists call the anthers—one, then another, then another, looking, as the old man had predicted, very weary and perhaps a little bored, from the task of hurling millions of enterprising bridegrooms into the tentative, plumelike embrace of an invisible and fastidious bride who should in her own time choose one. They lay there, the three cupids, sort of hanging out, with their heads in their hands, saying plainly the ceremony was over.

"The honeymoon comes afterward," said Weaver. "Nobody may see that."

They all stood up. Dreadwind looked around and was surprised to see that the appearance of the wheat had wonderfully changed. Then he realized that what he had been watching on one stalk had been taking place everywhere at the same time. The whole field was in flower.

As they came back to the road Weaver's manner of

a sudden changed for the worse. Dreadwind walked
at Cordelia's side. That may have been it. Several
attempts on Dreadwind's part to make conversation
the old man rebuffed either by silence or a sultry excla-
mation. When they came to the gate where father and
daughter had turned in the night before they turned
again in the same way, with this difference, that the old
man did not speak and the girl looked back.

Dreadwind began to search the circumstances for
some pretext on which to continue seeing them. Not
them of course, but one of them. And the question
was not whether he should see her again, or why; it
was only how. The impulse that had brought him to
the wheat fields was off the track, ditched, abandoned
upside down. A different locomotive now was pulling
his train. By the same road he had come he walked
back to the town, and saw only as much of the landscape as his feet touched, and that dimly. What he did
in the town was to buy an automobile out of a dealer's
window and spend the afternoon learning to drive it.
Then he clothed himself to new purpose, drove in the
evening to the house where they were, walked up the
door and asked for them—for Weaver.

And they were gone. She was gone!

Their going, he was told, had nothing strange about
it; that was their whimsical way. They would come
with one wind and go with another. Nevertheless, it
was sudden. Yes, a little more so than usual. No,
they did not say where they were going. They never
did say. Right after dinner, the midday meal in the
country, they calmly departed. At first Dreadwind

suspected that the woman who stood in the doorway telling him this was evasive. As he became convinced of her sincerity he was bewildered.

"Have you known them long?" the woman asked.

Dreadwind said he hadn't, but did not disclose how very slight his acquaintance with them was.

"Then you wouldn't know," said the woman. "They appear and disappear that way, like migratory birds, as my mother said, only of course it's strange—the two of them so. As long as we've lived here, it's now going on eight years, they've come every year. They never stopped with us before. I don't mean we wouldn't be glad to have them again."

"How do they live?" Dreadwind asked.

"By this and that and what the Lord provides," said the woman. "Anyone is glad to have them, as I say, especially if it's about harvest time. The girl helps indoors. Him? You'd have to ask the men what he does. I can't exactly say. It's what he knows, I reckon. Once I heard him preach a funeral. Naturally he would get something for that. He can cure animals, they say, and take spells off."

She stopped and began to regard Dreadwind in a quizzical manner, with some slyness in it.

"I don't think you'll find them," she said.

"Why not."

"So many roads going every which way," she said.

"That isn't what you meant," said Dreadwind. "Why do you think I won't find them?"

"Well, maybe you can," she said, of the first opinion

still. "I'd certainly tell you how if I knew myself. He's very suspicious."

"Of whom?" asked Dreadwind.

"I'm sure I don't know," said the woman, pretending to be perfectly blank.

She knew the direction in which they had walked away. And that was all. Dreadwind thanked her and was halfway to the gate when the woman called to him as if she had forgotten something.

"Was she expecting you to ask for her?"

"I don't know," Dreadwind replied.

"Because you didn't ask for her, did you?" the woman continued. "You asked for him. She said if anybody asked for her to give them this."

She held out an envelope.

"Thank you," said Dreadwind, taking it. The envelope was sealed, but had no writing on it. Afterward it occurred to him that his claim to it had not been proved, not even asserted more so than by the act of reaching for it, and he wondered why the woman had made not the slightest difficulty about giving it to him.

A mile from the house he broke it open, and out of it fell a wheat spikelet in flower. There was nothing else.

CHAPTER V

IN the direction they had gone he drove to the
first crossroad and turned right. After many miles
in vain that way he came back to the point at which he
had turned right, and turned left. Returning again he
drove straight ahead to the next crossroad and went
first right and then left. In this manner he searched
the country methodically. Nobody had seen them.
They had passed without trace if they passed at all.

Thus a fortnight had elapsed when one morning
Dreadwind's quest was almost rewarded and then
immediately disappointed again in a very singular
manner.

He had spent the latter part of the night in the automobile, a little off the road, in a space screened on three
sides by a high wild hedge. He came awake as streaks
of light began to show in the east. For several moments he lay motionless, observing the sky. Suddenly
in a spectral manner a tall, lone figure appeared in the
road. He recognized it instantly as Weaver; and even
in that dim light he could see that the old man was in
extreme trouble with his thoughts. He would start,
stop, turn, walk up and down, and kept twisting his
hands together. Then he seemed to have resolved it,
for suddenly he left the road, leaped the ditch, and
stood in the edge of a field of wheat. From Dreadwind's angle of vision he was in silhouette above the

wheat and so exaggerated in stature that he seemed supernaturally tall, touching the sky. The whole omen of him was evil. Dreadwind had a flash of phantasy. He though of Abraham about to sacrifice his son, and shuddered.

What happened next was mysterious. Out of the depths of an inner garment the old man produced as it were a pouch or small sack, opened it, dipped his fingers therein and appeared to be casting an impalpable substance on the air. There was a fresh breeze blowing against the wheat and that of course would account in a natural way for what Dreadwind at this moment observed with a superstitious feeling—namely, that the wheat seemed to be running *from* Weaver, not toward him. Although he took rational note of the obvious physical explanation, still he could do nothing with the fancy that it was running from the old man in terror.

After Weaver had several times repeated the act of sowing something on the air, Dreadwind's curiosity moved him. He rose and approached. Weaver neither saw nor heard him. With only the ditch between them Dreadwind stopped and called his name.

The old man turned his face—only his face. Its expression was so calamitous, so mingled of pity, pain and cruel resolve, that Dreadwind was shocked. Before he could speak again, Weaver dropped the pouch and went stumbling away through the wheat, trampling it in a heedless manner and never once looked back. His walking down the wheat in that way, as if it were nonexistent or lifeless, so contrary to the feeling of

tenderness hitherto revealed, was a sight that unnerved
Dreadwind.   He said it was like an act of murder unconsciously committed.   When he had so far recovered
as to be able to act the old man was invisible.

The first thing he did was to pick up the abandoned
pouch.   It was still half full of some fine, brownish
stuff with a sick, unpleasant odor.   He put this away in
his pocket and then went about the neighborhood lei-
surely, making no inquiries at first, expecting to come
upon Weaver and Cordelia in a casual manner.   He
imagined that Weaver had not recognized him.   There
had been no sign of recognition in that extraordinary
expression; and this was all the more probable from
the fact that one of Weaver's peculiarities was a morbid longsightedness.   When he was in a state of feeling his eyes focused slowly and with difficulty upon
near-by objects.

But not only was there no trace of either Weaver or
Cordelia in the immediate vicinity; there was not a
house within a radius of many miles where they had
been seen.   Dreadwind was disagreeably astonished.
Elusiveness in this degree was adroit, not accidental.
Forebodings assailed him.   He began to have ugly
thoughts about Weaver.

And now it occurred to him to work backward.   The
woman who had delivered Cordelia's mute token might
know with whom they had stopped before coming to
her.   If she did, then in the same way others might be
able to refer him back, and so he would go from one
place to another until he had discovered their source.

Thus he came again to the house where all the be-

ginning was, and knocked—as by this time he had
learned to do—at the kitchen door. The woman's
name was Purdy. She was not surprised to see him
and seemed to be indulgently amused.

"I knew you wouldn't find them," she said before
Dreadwind had spoken.

No. She had no news of them. They had not been
back.

"Do you know where they were before coming
here?" Dreadwind asked.

"That won't do you any good," she said.

She had been making bread. There was dough on
her hands. She gathered it into a little ball and rolled
it thoughtfully between her palms.

"Perhaps not," said Dreadwind. "You've been right
so far, I'm sorry to say. However, I'd like to try."

She gave him the name of a family in the next
county, together with explicit directions about the way
to go, twice repeated.

"Now be sure you don't get lost," she called after
him. He turned to thank her again. "And stop again
if you are passing this way," she added.

He found the place. The migrants had passed four
days there, and to one side of the house it was a sore
matter. The woman lost her temper at the mention
of Weaver's name and denounced him for a witch. She
was more voluble than coherent. Presently her husband appeared, put her aside and stood himself in the
whole doorway. He wished to talk of womankind for
listening womankind's benefit. Dreadwind wished only
to know where the Weavers had been before this.

Gradually the man admitted the probability that they might have been with a family twelve miles south. Dreadwind was departing with this information. The man followed him to the gate and there created a man-to-man atmosphere, with no annotating female in the background.

Dreadwind, he said, would know what he meant. Women were not such as had judgment into them. They put on everything a man said and wore it hard around the house whether it was intended that way or not. Weaver was all right, only sometimes he had a strong way of saying things and it wasn't everybody knew how to take it.

Dreadwind asked what he had been saying here to jeopardize his welcome on the feminine side.

Things there wasn't anything into really, the man said. Things nobody would notice unless they put them on like women always done. Such as one morning at breakfast the woman said she dreamed of the devil and Weaver said you dreamed of the devil when you let the dishwater stand. There was nothing into that, was there? How did he know she let her dishwater stand? But the woman got mad and let herself go. Well, things like that. If you had short fingernails you was a tale bearer. If you kicked up your dress behind you was a thief. Maybe, maybe not. You would see many things that was both so and not so. What was so of a field might not be so of a furrow. Anyhow, it wasn't meant personal, like the woman took it, not even about the hair. He said if birds made a nest of your hair you went crazy. So ever since the woman was going about the place knocking birds' nests out of the trees and raking the grass for bits of her hair that might have blowed out of the house, thinking the old man put a spell on her mind. But as for him being a witch, it was like them inquisitors calling everybody heretics and burning them up because they couldn't understand what they said. Suppose he could talk with dumb animals, like he said. Wasn't that on account of him being born Christmas? And if he could read cobwebs and tell what the rest of the winter was going to be according to how the liver and spleen was pointed in a fresh-killed hog, that was knowledge. Whatever you might say it came out that way.

"Juknow," the man asked, eyeing Dreadwind keenly —"juknow why you never seen a blue jay on Friday and why on the first Thursday in July at two o'clock all the toads turn pink for thirty minutes?"

"Why?" said Dreadwind.

"Ask him," the man answered.

With that he was through. He became suddenly apprehensive. To further questions he returned evasive, suspicious monosyllables. Dreadwind offered to shake hands. The man hastily popped out of the gate.

"Never shake hands over a gate," he said.

At the next place, twelve miles south, there was a tidy woman who never let her dishwater stand and was careful of her hair. She had liked Cordelia and felt very sorry for her on the ground that in being so devoted to that old curmudgeon of a father she was throwing her life away. It seemed hardly natural, and such a lovely girl too. However, she said nothing

against Weaver directly. Her husband smiled vaguely,
a little uneasily, at some secret recollection of the old
man, saying: "He's a character all right."   Dreadwind said he had been told that Weaver was a kind of
witch who worked upon people's superstitions.

"Yes," said the man.   "He might do that.   But
you'll see there's generally some point to it.   There
are people you can't get at in any other way for their
own good.   There's a man near here that never fed
his stock properly.   Weaver told him at twelve o'clock
Christmas Eve cows kneel down and talk with the devil
in the language of the Old Testament and complain if
they haven't been used right.   And that was the reason
he had been having bad luck.   The man believed it.
Weaver nailed two brooms in a cross on the barn—you
can see them as you go by—and said they would keep
evil spirits away as long as the cows got enough to eat.
And he believed that.   It was good for the cows.
What's more, the man's having better luck."

"Anything else?" Dreadwind asked.

"He can find water with a peach twig," said the
man.   "I never took any stock in that myself until I
saw him do it right here on this place."

In that way and from place to place Dreadwind got
a lot of information he was not seeking, all of it interesting, and nothing to the main point.   Nobody
knew who Weaver was nor how it happened that he
came to be wandering over the wheat country year
after year with a beautiful daughter attached.   Their
trail was easy to follow in this backward fashion until
it jumped off the earth in Texas.   It appeared to have

started there, not once but several times, for people
remembered their coming again and again; only here
nobody knew whence they came or where they.had been
last. Here was their point of departure, it seemed,
but not their source; and Dreadwind was more mystified than ever.

He had been three times to see a family that was
said to have known the Weavers in a time long past.
The last member of the family had now denied it. The
clew was therefore false and Dreadwind was leaving
it.

Outside the gate in the shade of an ash tree, on a
little bench, sat a man who had long since ceased to
observe the world or mind its vanities. He had cut
it off. His hands were folded, his knees lay together,
his toes turned in, and the long, wonderful beard that
had absorbed his masculinity was tucked into his shirt
bosom. He seemed very little, very old and wholly
impenetrable. Dreadwind had noticed him before,
always in that place on the bench, remote and unseeing. You could imagine that without power, authority
or grandeur of any sort he lived there among his
progeny, begotten of himself and a strong woman, and
derived his dignity from the one phenomenon of ven-
erable silence; also that he took a great deal of ironic
pleasure in it.

"I don't suppose you knew Absalom Weaver?" said
Dreadwind, more out of curiosity to see how he would
react when directly provoked than with any sort of
expectation.

The patriarchal deposit did not stir. One could not

believe that anything within it stirred. Dreadwind stood looking down at it for a minute, then turned away and had one foot on the running board of his car when a far-away voice at the pitch of an unoiled hinge arrested him. The bearded figure had uttered words. Dreadwind asked him what they were. After a long time he repeated them.

"Ye can suppose it," he said.

"Well, do you?" Dreadwind asked.

"Better nor he knew himself," was the answer when at length it came.

Dreadwind sat down on the grass, facing the motionless figure, and gave the impulse plenty of time to augment itself.

"What made him a vagabond?" he asked.

"If you ask him why he don't own any land—if you ask him—do you know what he will say?"

"What will he say?" asked Dreadwind.

"He will say he ain't fit to own land. And he ain't fit."

"Why will he say that?" asked Dreadwind.

"I told him. I told him he were not fit to own land. And he ain't the one to forget it."

It was an afternoon's work, requiring much subtlety and patience, to mine that dry cavern of its treasure. Each fragment was parted with reluctantly. And it was a plain story, deserving to be briefly told.

CHAPTER VI

WEAVER, as one might have guessed, was once a farmer on his own land. He was a good farmer. No trouble there. He was industrious and far-seeing. No trouble yet. But he had a gambling mania. What he gained by farming he lost in the nearest bucket shop. He gambled in wheat. Never anything else. This went on for years. The mania grew. His betting losses in that phantom wheat on the blackboard began to be more than all the profit he could win from the soil; and the farm itself became involved in debt. Each time a new mortgage was necessary to pay up his losses and avoid a lawsuit the cruelties of the domestic scene were greater. You can see it. A woman in the rôle of martyr, taking advantage of a just grievance to balance off all petty scores, as almost any woman will. Children bewildered at first and then beginning to take sides. A proud and willful man who must storm it through to save his own ego and authority.

The woman said that he promised each time to stop. Almost for certain he never did. He wasn't one who would, nor one who, if he had, would have defaulted on his word; and yet, of course, a woman in these circumstances, saying each time she would never sign

again, could not be expected clearly to see the difference
between an ultimatum and a covenant. She understood he would cease gambling. How could he go on
if she meant what she said and would never sign again?
But that was an understanding arrived at in her mind
alone. Anyone who knows a gambler, one in whom
the passion is deep, can imagine what he was thinking.
It would not be necessary for her to sign another mortgage. He would beat the phantom wheat game and
clear the farm of debt. What ruins the gambler is not
ill luck. It is counting on the future to pay for the
past.

The sequel is foreseen. This little effigy of a patriarch with his beard flowing into his bosom like a lost
river was at that time an intimate friend of the family
—one who understood everything, one in whom the
wife confided, one who meddled when he dared and
still bore the scars of Weaver's scorn. He was there
this night, hot with the news he had got in town.
Weaver at last had lost the farm. There had been a
sudden fall in the price of wheat. It wiped him out.
What was worse, he owed the bucket shop so much
that even what was left of the farm would not satisfy
the debt. There would be a dead horse to pay for.
Therefore, the friend argued, it would be better now
for the two boys to come forward and take charge of
the family's future. They could not be sued for the
father's debt. With all his wisdom he persuaded the
wife to this line of conduct and admonished her to be
firm. When he ceased speaking, having said everything three times, the little clock on a bracket shelf

against the wall took up his exhortation. It was a little out of plumb, with an injured tick, and kept saying: *"Be firm, be firm, be firm."*

It was a winter night. Snow was falling. They sat in the kitchen—the sympathetic friend, the wife and four children. The chores were all done. A lantern on the floor by the door had not quite gone out and was fuming. Supper was over, except Weaver's, and his was on a plate in the oven. It had been kept warm for so long that it was already spoiled, and no one minded it any more. The wife's arms lay limp on the red tablecloth in the round shadow of the hanging coal-oil lamp. At the slightest unexpected sound she would start, take in her breath, then let it out again in a weary, reconciled sigh. The kind of a woman who secretly enjoys misery and aggrievedness because she can so easily dramatize it. A girl of sixteen was clearing up. She had to walk around two boys, almost grown, who surrounded the stove; and she did it without speaking.

A much younger girl stood alone at the window looking out. It was she who spoke and her voice was bright.

"There he is," she said. "I see him."

The wife swallowed, twitched the corners of her mouth, and looked at the family's friend, who silently repeated the admonition, "Be firm." The child at the window continued to look out. The others listened. They heard him drive in and open the barn door. Neither of the two boys stirred. A few minutes later they heard him close the barn door and began to hearken for his step on the back porch. It did not come.

"What's he doing?" the wife asked, speaking to the girl in the window.

"Walking around," she answered, not turning her face. Her voice had changed.

Several minutes passed in silence.

"Now what's he doing?" the wife asked.

Instead of answering the girl threw her arm across her face, leaned against the window frame and began to sob.

"Oh, that child!" the mother sighed. "Stella, do look. See what he's doing."

Stella was wiping a plate. She approached the window obliquely, intending to glance out in passing. What she saw caused her to stop and look again and then to stand gazing. The hand that was drying the plate went slower and slower round and stopped. Then she turned from the window, shaking her head, frowning.

"I don't know what he's doing." she said.

"Can you see him?"

"Yes."

"Well, then, what does he seem to be doing?"

"He seems to be hugging the trees," said Stella.

"Oh, dear! Oh, dear!" the mother aspirated. "That's it. That's it."

"What's it, mother?" Stella asked in a petulant voice.

"Hush, child. Don't ask me. Will that young one stop her crying?"

Just then Weaver's steps were heard on the porch. The doorlatch clicked. He paused on the threshold and looked around him, at each of them in turn, at the room, at the familiar objects in it, as if he were trying to remember something. Then he picked up the fuming lantern, put it out and set it on the floor again. Forgetting to close the door or to remove his hat and outer coat he walked mechanically to the oven and drew forth his plate of supper without looking at it. He put it on the table, seated himself, and began to stare at it, as he had stared at everything else. Stella laid a knife and fork by his plate, holding herself aloof. He might have been a stranger. Nobody spoke to him. Then he seemed to see the food for the first time, or to become aware of it as food, and pushed it away with a gesture of distaste. The girl in the window was all this time regarding him with a stricken expression. The ticking of the clock became very loud. Weaver heard it. They were greatly mystified to see him go to the stove and begin thoughtfully to search the woodbox on the floor. He found a small splinter, whittled it a little and fitted it under the low side of the clock, making it plumb. Instantly, of course, its fickle heart changed. It ceased exhorting the wife to *"be firm, be firm, be firm,"* and began contentedly to murmur, *"that's it, that's it, that's it."* On the wall was a picture of Maud S. in a fluted walnut frame, crossed at the corners with carved butterflies. For a long time Weaver stood looking at that. Then he looked at his wife, took a step toward her, and stopped as one who remembered a hurt. What could he say? He was not one to repent, promise òr pray. He turned toward the door and was walking out. And it was then the family's friend spoke his mind out heroically. He had no way of understanding a man who in guilty circumstances would not grovel and stultify himself with explanations.

"Absalom Weaver," he said, "land is for them that's fit to own land. You ain't fit. That's why you've lost it. You ain't fit for anything, nor be you sorry."

Weaver was already in the open doorway, going out. He turned and spat on the floor.

"That's what I do when I cross a snake's trail," he said. "I spit in it." Then he went out, closing the door behind him. The family's friend ever afterward believed this act was a sign of how deeply his weak little shaft went in. He reared his pride upon it.

The natural dramatic period is never completely realized. Something unexpected happens. There was now a stir in the kitchen. The youngest child, no longer weeping, had taken her little coat down from its peg and was getting into it and pulling on her arctics at the same time. Everyone sensed what she meant to do; and no one spoke. Without stopping to fasten her arctics she snatched up her knitted cap and mittens and rushed headlong out of the door in pursuit of her father. That the mother made no gesture to restrain her seems at first a little strange, and yet it is naturally explained. Secretly, perhaps not admitting it to herself, she must have realized that Weaver's exit was final. Trust a silly woman to know her own man's folly. Secretly, too, she wished it so, and because she wished it she could not acknowledge it. In permitting the child to run after him she proved to herself that she did not know and did not wish it. Afterward she was able to say, even to believe, that she supposed he was going for a walk in the night, as he often did, and would bring her child back. And thus she was provided with a monstrous grievance—namely, that he never did.

"From that day to this Absalom Weaver's been walking to and fro in the earth, and the girl with him," said the absurd little primate who sat in the shade of the ash tree. He clicked in his beard with a malevolent sound, like a mechanical toy shutting up. He had done his worst. There the delation ended.

"How long ago was that?" Dreadwind asked.

"Nineteen years and five months."

"And how old was the girl that went with him?"

"Ten."

Dreadwind reflected. That would make Cordelia's age nearly thirty. And he had thought her still a girl. Her age thrilled him. Thirty! A proper age. Thirty, with the look of youth. A miracle reserved for him!

One more question. It was malicious, therefore he held it until the very end. "Did you marry Mrs. Weaver?" he asked.

Until then, through all that recital, only the lips of the patriarch had moved. Now the fingers twitched and the knees trembled. There seemed for a long time no likelihood of an answer. But it did come.

"She died," he said.

That was his last utterance. Not another word could be got out of him.

Now Dreadwind retraced his steps. There was nothing else to do. He was thinking he knew everything about them except how to find them when suddenly he remembered that pouch of brownish vile powder. He had left the stuff at the state agricultural laboratory to be analyzed. Forebodings assailed him as he stopped to get the report. The plant biologist on seeing him behaved in a constrained manner and referred him to the executive secretary of the bureau. That person scrutinized Dreadwind suspiciously and produced the laboratory's report with an ominous air. But instead of showing it he sat for a long time looking at it himself, tapping his foot against his desk, unable to decide how to act.

"Where did you get this stuff?" he asked.

Dreadwind said he had found it at the roadside in a pouch.

"You didn't bring it here in a pouch. You brought it in a paper."

Dreadwind said he had thrown the pouch away.

"Why?"

"Because I didn't like the look and smell of it," said Dreadwind, beginning to realize that he needed his wits. The last thing in the world he meant to do on any account was to involve Weaver in serious trouble. And this was evidently about to become serious. His answer was perhaps technically true. He had thrown the pouch away as an instinctive precaution. Even so, he could say that he liked not the smell and look of it. Then he was asked if he knew of any person having a possessory relation to the pouch? Had he seen anyone drop it? That was coming too close.

"I'm not to be interrogated in this grand-jury manner," he said, affecting to be irritated. "I found this stuff by the roadside, as I have said, and I was curious to know what it was. So I brought it to you. That's quite simple, isn't it? I don't know yet what it is, and since I took the trouble to bring it to you I'd like to know."

"It's rust," said the secretary, bluntly reacting; "the germinating principle of wheat rust."

"I've heard of rust," said Dreadwind, "but I don't know exactly what it is. Tell me, please."

"Rust," said the secretary, "is the common name for a parasitic fungus that attacks and destroys wheat. It multiplies with incredible rapidity from spores, somewhat like mushrooms, if you know. There is black rust and red rust. This stuff is the seed—that is to say, the spore—of black rust. Enough to kill half the wheat in Kansas. I never saw anything like it. The spores do not naturally occur in this concentrated way. Someone must have gathered or cultivated the stuff for a felonious purpose."

"If I come across any more of it I'll know what to do," said Dreadwind, and departed.

This, then, was the explanation of Weaver's excitement and tragic manner that morning when Dreadwind surprised him in the act of spreading the powder on the air.

He was killing the wheat!

But how was Weaver himself to be explained? One day kneeling in ecstasy at the foot of a wheat stalk to observe the nuptial ceremony!—another day sowing black death upon it! Dreadwind kept seeing him first in one act and then in the other; and these were as the acts of separate persons, one a mystic, the other a monster. And this was also Cordelia's father! He grew sick from thinking of it.

It was natural that his thoughts of Cordelia should associate with Mrs. Purdy, who had been the one and only point of contact. He liked the woman. He remembered her smile. There was knowing in it; also a little teasing and that slightly roguish, sweetly ironic air with which a woman looks on at these matters, as at a play wherein she has more of the secret than the actors and enjoys their silly confusion. He went to see her again. Nearly three weeks had gone by.

"I was passing," he explained.

"Oh," she said with a certain inflection. "Won't you come in."

She seemed more friendly, more knowing; and without asking if he was hungry she began to set the table and prepare food. It was mid-afternoon.

He watched her for a while without speaking. Her movements were quick and deft. Just to sit there under her ministrations was a soothing experience. Also for some reason it was reassuring. She knew Cordelia. Was that it? And with all her archness she was sympathetic.

"Are you sure the envelope she left was meant for me?" he asked.

"Weren't you?" she answered, bending over the stove.

"But how will she ever know I got it?" he said.

The food was ready. Mrs. Purdy put it before him. Then she made a trip to the spring house for butter. With putting the butter on the table she sat down herself, and said, looking at him steadily, "She knows you got it."

"What!" said Dreadwind. "How did she find it out?"

"I shouldn't have told you," said Mrs. Purdy. "Will you have some jelly?"

"Why shouldn't you have told me?"

"Shouldn't have," she said with a puckered mouth, shaking her head.

"Has she been here?" asked Dreadwind.

"What a pity, now, you couldn't have been passing three days ago," said Mrs. Purdy.

"Was she alone?"

"Who?"

"Cordelia. Was her father with her?"

"When?"

"Three days ago."

"My, how you do pin a body down," said Mrs. Purdy. "Have I said she was here three days ago? I only said what a pity you couldn't have been passing."

Dreadwind could see that she meant in the end to tell him. And whether she told him all or less, she gave him more than she knew. Cordelia had been discovered at daylight, sitting alone on a bench in the front yard.

"That round bench under the apple tree?" he asked.

Mrs. Purdy nodded. Of course; there was no other bench. What more commonplace object in the world than a bench? Yet suppose it happens to mark the point in space where the lines of two lives, infinitely predetermined through all the chances of matter, have crossed for the first time. That was the bench on which he sat down beside her in the lantern light. It was there she gave him her name. Mrs. Purdy knew nothing of this. She paused for a moment and studied him when he mentioned it; but she saw nothing in it and went on. They had found her there at daylight in a kind of reverie. Nobody knew when she came. She had been weeping. A woman could guess it. But she was not sad, except in the way one might sometimes like to be sad. And she was lovely. Mrs. Purdy would say it herself. She said it twice, noting the effect upon Dreadwind. They had asked her to stop for breakfast, and she couldn't, because her father would presently miss her. What she wished to know from Mrs. Purdy was whether anyone had asked for her. If not she would like her envelope back.

"Did she seem pleased to know it had been delivered?" Dreadwind asked.

"She was relieved," said Mrs. Purdy, a little severely, slowly choosing her word.

"And she left no message?" Dreadwind asked.

Mrs. Purdy frowned, hesitated, thought better of something she had been about to say, and continued: "What the girl really wanted was to tell me about a dream that worried her. This was the dream: There were two great vines. One she knew and the other she had forgotten the name of. Both had twined themselves around her. She did not mind that. She would have liked it, in fact, only that each one struggled to tear her from the other and without meaning to do so they were hurting her terribly. She kept saying to them, 'It is unnecessary! So unnecessary!' But neither one would listen. With that she woke up. She had dreamed this many times and it was giving her great anxiety."

"Did she wish you to tell me her dream?" asked Dreadwind.

Mrs. Purdy disdained to reply or to look at him, but rose suddenly and began clearing off the table with an acrimonious air, like the gust of wind that comes suddenly aboard ship and causes everything movable to slap and bang in a warning manner.

"Would it be possible for me to get a message to her through you?" asked Dreadwind, rising.

"It would not," she answered, going on with her work. Relenting a little she added: "She won't be back. She was sure of that."

"And you have no way of reaching her?"

"No more than you have," she answered over her shoulder.

"Thank you," he said, holding out his hand.

Then she looked at him, relented a little more, and they shook hands. She followed him slowly toward the door. On the threshold he looked back. She was gazing at him.

"They follow the harvest," she said. "That's all I can tell you."

"Why do you look at me as if—as if—I had forgotten something?" he asked.

"You haven't forgotten anything and I'm not looking at you," she said. "I'm only thinking."

"What are you thinking of?"

"Of what happens to women," she said, and turned away. The last he heard of her was a clangor of stove lids.

They followed the wheat. Well, then—there was nothing else for him to do.

And now you have him, to the eye, an aimless vagabond, wandering up and down the wheat country, sometimes sauntering, sometimes in haste, making inquiries so guardedly that almost nobody would have guessed he had a purpose at all, much less that impatience consumed him. It had occurred to him on reflection that hitherto his search had been too undisguished. Weaver might have heard of it.

By intuition he followed that magical wave of green-gold color the first sheen of which is seen by early June in Texas. Thence, adding mass and weight and glory to itself, it travels by two movements. One is whimsical and zigzag, determined by the local weather and where the captured sunlight comes here a little sooner ripe than there. The other one is stately and momentous, tending always north.

Dreadwind noticed that as the wheat changed color from green to golden opalescence, change was everywhere in everything — the sky, the light, the insect hymn, even in the ways of people. Men became distraught and anxious.

It is a time of crisis. There is gladness in the sight of plenty, yet this is strangely tinged with melancholy. Why is that? Why were people always sad about a harvest, therefore having recourse to festivals and merry-making? Perhaps because finalities are sad. What was soft and lithe and lovely now is dry and brittle, fixed in momentary splendor. The steel is whetted. The hand that raised it up must also cut it down. Life contains death and will not accept the fact. The wheat complains. Its whispering voice is now grown old, petulant and querulous. The heads are heavy and seem to toss about in pain.

Dreadwind must have made a very strange figure against that background. But whereas at first he had been much noticed and stared after, now his appearance, sometimes in most unexpected circumstances, excited no surprise. This was another change. Partly it was owing to the nervous tension peculiar to the atmosphere of ripening wheat. The farmer at this time becomes absent-minded. His thoughts are on the wheat and he does not know what he is thinking. He has an amazed impersonal attitude toward the event, as if a field of grain crying:

> *Cut me, cut me;*
> *I am brittle.*
> *Cut me, cut me;*
> *Hurt me little,*

were not his own, not a thing a man had done, but a revealed episode, natural because it recurs and none the less mysterious for that reason. His last act at night is to look at it again. At daybreak he will be seen walking in it. Here and there he plucks a head, breaks it open, examines it, smells it, tries the kernel with his finger nail and then with his teeth. All the time his eye is anxiously watching the weather. It may come on to rain or to blow or to do both. Nothing is certain. If he is religious he will pray and make vows. If he is superstitious he will look for signs and omens and secretly perform little rites of propitiation. As who would not?

The great task of modern civility is to create and sustain an artificial environment expressly designed to eliminate the savage uncertainties of natural existence. Within that artificial environment, besides security, there is foretelling. Nothing is left to chance; nothing is miraculous. Industry no longer relies upon wind and rainfall—that is, upon the whims of nature for the power to turn its wheels. When the ironmaster pours ore, fuel, limestone and chemicals into the top of a blast furnace he need not pray for a good run of metal. He knows precisely what the iron will be because its qualities are predetermined by scientific chemistry. He hath dispensed with the Lord. So with every physical process in all that world of machines and laboratories from which mischievous, meddlesome deities have been cast out.

But the farmer who feeds this world has no artificial environment. He stands alone facing the elemental rhythms. They are uncontrollable, unpredictable. He may know plant biology, he may know the chemistries of soil and vegetation, he may be as scientific as the Department of Agriculture could wish him to be, and yet the wind will blow when and how it listeth, the rain will fall by a law of its own, the sun hath no preoccupation with the weal of mankind. In all nature there is no forethought for civilization.

The cities are either ignorant or contemptuous of this fact. They are walled about, not with walls of stone as before, but with the barriers of the applied sciences. They know not how their food is produced nor whence it comes. Somewhere in the world the sun will shine; somewhere the rain will fall. They have ships and railroads to bring their food from any distance and the gold wherewith to pay for it. One's dinner in New York may represent Canadian sunlight converted into wheat and South American sunlight changed into beef, and one may not only never know it; one never even thinks of it.

Thus in modern circumstances it is the farmer alone who carries on the struggle in a natural environment, subject to the hazards of season, weather, sunspots, mysterious cycles of injurious life. He belongs to a race apart. We have forgotten the language in which he thinks.

Well, another reason why Dreadwind in his going about began to be less noticed was that his figure was swallowed up in that tide of human miscellany which rises each year in Oklahoma and follows the sickle bar north to the end of the harvest.

The annual migration of reapers is one of the oldest proceedings in the world. In romantic times it

occurred over limited areas in a naïve, spontaneous
manner.   Ruth came out of the land of Moab to Beth-
lehem in the beginning of the barley harvest.   That
was a great way to walk and really no distance at all.
Now with railroads and steamships it may be organized massively on economic lines, and sometimes is, as
when shiploads of Italians go each year from Italy's
winter to South America's summer and return when the
Argentine crop is by.   Every month in the year is
harvest time somewhere in the world.   Italian grain
ripens in June; Argentine wheat is ripe in December.

There are places where the migration can still be
picturesque.   But with us the spirit is almost forgotten.
Nowhere else is the harvest horde so accidental, so un-
festive, so ephemeral in structure, so dissimilar in its
elements.   It has no common character, no place of
origin, no existence before or after; and when you
think what would happen if it did not appear like a
self-evolved phenomenon at the appointed time and
place you wonder again how people in the cities can
take their food for granted.   And yet it has never
quite failed.   It were a pity if it did.

The life is nomadic and free, the wages are clear,
humanity is level and the work is a series of sudden
exploits.   Nor is this tale of inducements the full per-
suasion.   The call of the harvest is something you feel.
It reaches down to the earth sense in men, to blood-
and-tissue memories of exciting primeval festivals,
myth rites, ancient forms of nature worship; to
memories of the feast of Pentecost, of sacrificing to
Ceres, of how the fearsome Druids celebrated the

ingathering, of the reapers' kern baby, of cutting the mare, of the maiden sheaf, of the Roman saturnalia at the end of the vintage when amid universal rejoicing and license even the slaves were free and ate at the master's table.

Long after people began to gather in cities the response to this great ground call was universal and served two needs. One was the instinctive human need for contact with the earth. The other was the need of agriculture for extra hands when the grain is ripe and must be taken quickly. Thus for a great while the city performed an ideal function. It absorbed the surplus labor of the country at other times and released it for the harvest. But on the rise of modern industrialism, with its fixity of special tasks, all this use and custom fell. Hence new social problems in the city from a thwarting of the ground instinct; hence also the resort of agriculture to labor-saving power machinery.

The call has never changed. Only now so many live amid the ceaseless din of wheels and tools that millions never hear it. They would not know it if they did. Those who do respond are the unreconciled. Actually the number is large. Relatively it is small— that is to say, small and diminishing in relation to the vaster growing number in whom the instinct is frustrate; small again in relation to the magnitude of the work performed. In all the cities of the world two or three hundred years ago there would not have been labor enough to harvest by hand in our time one North American wheat crop. Machinery does it. The shapeless, self-mobilized body of men that appears each year where and when the sheen of green-gold color begins to show, that fastens upon it, that devours it utterly so that nothing is left but a dead pale stubble, is really symbolic. What does it symbolize? The vestige of a custom we have perhaps done very ill to part with. A blind triumph of machine power. A transition completed. A problem unsolved. And we treat it as a casual economic fact! Harvest labor, we say, governed by the law of supply and demand. It comes when it is wanted, perhaps not because it is wanted but for another reason, and disperses itself. When the harvest is ended it will vanish away.

To an eye above this economic fact might resemble a multiple animal, headless and eyeless, with some power of peristaltic locomotion, an unerring instinct for the color on which it feeds, one common belly and myriad mouths, each mouth equipped with a highly destructive mechanism. These innumerable mouth mechanisms, one on each tentacle of the animal, are what produce that droning, ominous sound. If the mind behind the eye above were given to reflection it might deduce from what it sees a perfect theory of evolution. Formerly this reaping animal made no sound at all, seeming rather to work by stealth with sharp sickle teeth, and was so much smaller and less voracious that only a painstaking observer would know it for the same species of thing. The conclusion would be that it had increased thus in size and effectiveness because the stuff on which it feeds became for some unknown reason much more abundant on the face of the earth.

But to its own eye this animal resembles nothing so complex and fanciful. It sees itself simply as a band of diverse individuals united for a time in the task of driving through the wheat fields mechanical beasts—that is to say, automatic reapers, binders and threshers. And that of course is as we see it. We take everything for granted, including the mechanical beasts all evolved from the sickle, the greatest of which is called a combine, moving under its own power on wheels eight feet high, devouring a swath forty feet wide, cutting, threshing, cleaning and sacking the wheat as it goes, in one continuous operation. Tending these beasts is increasingly the work of the harvest hand.

If it seems less romantic than when grain was cut with a blade on a crooked stick and threshed under the feet of oxen, that is so. But if it seems less thrilling that is because wonder moves only in mysteries and man is not mystified by his own inventions. No deity ever thought to create a harvesting machine. That one could have done it, had one thought of it, is open to doubt.

Even yet among the migrant reapers you will find skilled farmers. They are needed on the smaller farms, where the wheat on being cut is first shocked or stacked to be threshed afterward—men who know how to build and cap a shock to make it wind and weather proof. These are the landless ones who hunger for it. Some are tragic, worthy only to be hired. They reap in envy. Others are peasant immigrants hither blown by winds of hope. They will presently take root. But in the modern harvest, owing to the use of power machinery, much of the work requires no special farming skill. Almost anyone may turn his hand raw to it. Hence in that sprawling procession, which to the eye above would resemble a monstrous, devouring organism, one will find tramps, casual vagabonds, preachers, artisans, college students, anæmics in quest of health, criminals in hiding, foreigners, derelicts, poets, artists, strife bringers, thieves, old wives and new at the cook shacks with numerous self-preserving progeny appended. The scene has many aspects and there are many ways of viewing it. There are ways to view it profitably. The men who do this do nothing else. They look with keen, appraising eyes, seem never to be in haste, give no account of their errand and are always passing. Dreadwind, to whom everything else was strange, knew a good deal about these men. He identified them at once. Not as individuals. He had never seen them before. But he knew what they were doing and whose instruments they were.

They were the eyes of the wheat pit.

CHAPTER VII

AS a timber looker by walking through a forest and sighting it with his eyes may guess very accurately how many board feet of lumber it will cut, so these crop experts who go ceaselessly to and fro in the wheat, observing its growth, charting its area, comparing its conditions, detecting rust and blight, are believed to be able to estimate the total yield in bushels.

Seldom does it happen that any two of them agree. There is no difficulty in that fact. It is rather better that they should disagree, for then as their reports are received in the wheat pit and telegraphed simultaneously to thousands of offices all over the country where people sit in front of blackboards betting on the rise and fall of prices there is the excitement of contrary opinion; gambling is stimulated. Violent controversies arise. One expert, who last year was right when the United States Department of Agriculture was wrong, says there will be a big crop; rumors of damage have been exaggerated for reasons which he will not demean himself to characterize as they deserve. And the Board of Trade house that employs him swears to this and advises its clients to sell wheat for a fall. Another expert, who does not pretend to be infallible but whose record for five years has been such that one who had bet on his conclusions consistently would have

gained all the money in the world—he says the crop
will be short, no matter what faked-up estimates to the
contrary are put out by whom he forbears to name;
and the Board of Trade house that employs him urges
its clients to buy for a rise.

Thus speculation in phantom wheat is fomented.
That is the main thing. Why else should Board of
Trade houses hire experts to estimate the wheat crop?

Those clients who sit in rows before the blackboards
are like leaden lumps if you let them alone. They
cannot make up their own minds. Act upon them with
suggestion and they become golden geese. They neither sow in righteousness nor reap in mercy. Few of
them would know a field of wheat from a patch of
alfalfa. Yet in the course of a year they will buy and
sell twenty bushels of phantom wheat for each bushel
of real wheat produced by the labor of two and a
half millions of farmers. In order that they shall do
this they must be supplied with suggestions. Hence
these private crop experts, hired by the proprietors of
the blackboards, to keep the speculative mind in a
state of futile anxiety.

The Department of Agriculture also estimates the
crop. But its reports are issued once a month. That
is not often enough. What would speculation do between times? Besides, the private experts always disagree with the government experts, and this adds zest
to the blackboard betting.

A more painstaking and very secretive type of expert was new to Dreadwind. He represented neither
private speculators in the wheat pit nor the proprietors

of blackboards with their little pens of golden geese. His employer was the hard-minded miller; and it was his extraordinary business to know what was in the wheat—in the kernels of the wheat.

The chemical content of wheat varies with soil and local weather. In an area where growing conditions have been exceptionally favorable—where, for example, there has been by chance just the right amount of rainfall, the precious gluten content may be higher than in wheat on similar soil in the next neighborhood, though it all looks precisely alike. The difference is invisible and yet very important. The miller's expert works intensively. He marks those areas where for special reasons the gluten content is likely to run high and watches them tenderly. When threshing begins he takes from each area a little sample and rushes it off to a laboratory to be analyzed.

If the chemical examination confirms his expectations the miller is informed that wheat in this particular place contains a premium percentage of gluten. Does the miller then instruct his agent to buy that wheat at a premium price? No, indeed. He enters the fact on his working record. He knows what the wheat contains and to what elevators the farmers who grew it will bring it for sale and storage. In due time he needs such wheat to mix with other wheat, and when he does he orders a few carloads from the local elevator in one of those high-gluten areas—orders just the common grade at the common price and nobody knows the difference. Thus the millers, thanks to the work of their experts, are able to fish premium wheat out of the great No. 2 stream and pay only the average price.

*   *   *

"And what's the matter with that?" said Moberly with a snort. "How will a miller know where the gluten is unless he finds it for himself? The farmer might analyze his own wheat. But he won't. And when the miller has found it it has already cost him enough."

"I've nothing to argue," I said. "I'm telling you, as he told me, how Dreadwind saw the harvest."

"Meanwhile the needle is lost in the straw," said Goran, groaning. "We've got to learn all about straw before we can find the lovely object. If I didn't know it had been found by the way the story started I'd go to bed now. How? That's what I want to hear."

"You'd better hear what happened to Dreadwind," I said; "how he saw more than appears in the harvest and what construction he put upon it. Otherwise you cannot understand the change in him. I remember he said just at this point that all his life in the city he had been asking himself a certain question. It arose from the theatrical spectacle of spending. Everywhere this spending—silly, wasteful, competitive, imitative spending, until many were bored with it, wanting nothing and spending more. Shops more magnificent than ancient temples, all dedicated to this worship. Miles of lighted streets frantically jammed with spenders. Where did they get it? That was the question. Somebody had to pay for all this spending. He never could see who the payers were. He was a spender, you see. He produced nothing and yet he could spend. How and by what right? Perhaps the question arose really not from the spectacle as he thought; he had got to wondering about himself. Well, now he began to see. The farmer was one who paid. There might be others also. The farmer certainly paid. Everyone who touched him made him pay. The whole modern affair was organized against him. What he sold he sold on the buyer's terms. What he bought he bought on the seller's terms. That was all you needed to know about him, Dreadwind said. One in that situation was bound to be exploited. People could not help exploiting him. It was not a conspiracy. It was a condition. Imagine trusting human nature not to take advantage of the seller who asks, 'How much will you give?' Imagine trusting it not to take advantage of the buyer who asks, 'How much will you take?' "

"Rotten nonsense," said Moberly. "A farmer's a farmer. That's all you need to know about him. He doesn't know any better. If he did he wouldn't be a farmer."

"Yes, he said that, too," I answered; "almost in those words—that the farmer was what was left. The talent he wants is attracted away in the gristle and trained on the other side to be used against him. He spoke of you, Moberly. He said you were the most skillful grain manipulator in the world. You were born on a farm. Did you remain there? No. Instead of developing your extraordinary skill of trade

in the farmer's behalf you went over to the other side
—to the buyer's side."

Moberly snorted.   "What do you mean by the
buyer's side?" he demanded.

"I don't mean anything.   Are you asking me what
Dreadwind meant?"

"What does anybody mean by that?" he asked.
"One side or another.   There is no one side.   Grain
is handled in a two-sided market place like any other
merchandise, or like securities on the Stock Exchange.
There is buying, and there is selling, neither without
the other.   A trader must work on both sides."

"Obviously," I answered.   "Only Dreadwind called
my attention to a fact I had never thought of before.
The Stock Exchange, for example, is a seller's market.
It is organized and conducted from the seller's point
of view—in the interest of those who create securities
for sale.   Therefore the paramount effort is to keep
prices as high as possible against the buyer.   But the
Board of Trade is a buyer's market.   Its machinery
was designed and is controlled in the buyer's interest—
that is, in the interest of those who buy and consume
grain.   Therefore the dominant motive is to keep
prices as low as possible, to the seller's disadvan-
tage."

"It isn't so," said Moberly, speaking without reflection.

"But it is," said Selkirk, who had not spoken before.
"It is so," he added, exquisitively tapping the ashes
from the end of his cigarette.   "I shall never forget
it."

"Is this a tale at all?" sighed Goran. "Did your reflective hero, this Mr. Dreadwind, now living with a haunted tree in Burma—did he ——?"

"No. He did not."

*   *   *

CHAPTER VIII

THAT wave of green-gold color breaks in Canada. There the harvest ends. The reapers disappear. One September day Dreadwind parked a worn-out car by a little railroad station in the province of Alberta and bought a ticket for Chicago.

His office was one little room in a high corner of the Eyrie Building. With the act of inserting the key he remembered having closed the door. It had not turned on its hinges since. Everything would be as he left it; and yet nothing would be the same. He was vaguely aware of some fundamental change. Closing the door had been like the careless farewell which turns out to have been the parting forever; and opening it again was the sudden discovery.

Nearly four months had elapsed. All that had happened in that time flashed across his inner vision in one momentous picture. He was one of those rare persons whose memory restores the scene itself in full color so that it seems actually to be viewed again. Most of us are able to retrace only the faintest outline of things in black and white. He saw himself as an actor in that picture, sitting with Cordelia in those first moments under the apple tree on the lantern-lighted lawn, then kneeling with her in the wheat field at dawn, then pursuing her.

There was a nonexistent moment in which he almost saw her where he had not seen her, clairvoyantly. So he believed.

What really occurred to him in that imaginary interval on the threshold of his office was much more thrilling than any mental presentment of her image. I am telling you this. He could not say it. There came to him in that instant an aching physical sense of her existence, as of something that had never been realized before, originally wonderful. With that experience came also the clear and astonishing perception of another reality. A very singular fact this was. When he closed the door he had been alone in the world, a free and solitary person, preferring that state above any other. Now that was no longer so. He was not alone, nor did he wish to be.

The hour of day was one o'clock. He pushed the door open. On the floor were some letters. He stirred them with his foot and did not pick them up. The ticker by the window was running without tape. All this time it had been running without tape, producing a phantom record of a phantom thing. How appropriate! He wondered where the dust came from— how it could get into a closed room—and began absently to trace a pattern in it on the flat surface of his desk. The pattern was—CCCCC. Then seeing what he did he smiled and with his handkerchief wiped the top of the desk.

He shook the handkerchief in the air and used it again to rough-clean the little wooden object he had picked up with the other hand. This was a rudely carved bear, about four inches high, with an absurd and friendly leer. Its history is worth knowing. As a lonesome boy in Wall Street he used to pass it night and morning in a curio dealer's window and gradually invested it with a superstitious phantasy. With the proceeds of his first tiny gambling transaction in the bucket shop where he worked he went and bought it for two dollars and it became, I believe, his only permanent possession. It was both a luck idol and the symbol of his practice as a speculator.

Now, having dusted it off, with a kind of abusive affection, he put it down again in the middle of the desk and stood for a long time gazing alternately at it and then around the room. Nothing else in the room seemed in any way personal. Everything else had first to be remembered, like the things one sees on coming awake in strange surroundings. The past has to be recreated, up to the moment of having gone to sleep.

Dreadwind's past came back to him slowly. It was not merely that a certain experience discontinuous with his past and perhaps incompatible therewith had befallen him. Here was another kind of fact. What he had been he no longer was and could not be again. This was not a decision, not a matter of resolve, not a conclusion arrived at by reflection. It was simply so. How it came to be so he did not know. There in front of him lay the memorandum in his own handwriting of his last transactions in the pit. He had been a wheat gambler. Yes. But he knew that he should never make another bet in the wheat pit. Why? He did not know why. And it was not until he had dusted off the little bear and sat there communing with it that he knew it at all. There was no moralizing about it. There was only the finality.

*   *   *

"How extraordinary!" said Selkirk, in a tone of soliloquy.

"In what aspect?" I asked.

He replied slowly: "That a man's luck idol should tell him when to quit."

*   *   *

Of course, gambling is full of these concealed superstitions. It would be so. There is no way of accounting for luck beyond the simple rule of three. In its runs and wanton freaks it is totally mysterious; and its votaries may believe anything, not because what they believe is of itself probable, but because the mind cannot rest in a state of disbelief. It is necessary to believe that one believes something. Every successful gambler walks with the dread that his luck will turn, or, worse still, that it will leave him without warning. He will think it is only willful, prankish, that it is teasing him, when in fact it has turned its back, and this he is seldom aware of until it is too late.

Some will imagine that Dreadwind's funny little idol warned him to quit. Others will suppose that he had some intuition about it. That has happened—a man having all of a sudden the very definite feeling his touch is gone, without being able either to analyze the feeling or say what it is he has lost. The feeling is a fact, and though the rest of it were wholly imaginary it would be dangerous, even fatal, for that man to go on. The feeling of having lost his way with chance would wreck his play. These are matters of dark subtlety. We really know nothing about them. What Dreadwind himself thought would be of no importance. The subject himself is always one who has never rationalized his own acts. He never can tell how his mind works. He finds himself here or there and cannot say how he came. His mental processes are unconscious. Conclusions occur to him, complete and final, charged with impulse. They demand to be translated forthwith into action; and they are.

However, it seems to be true that he thought nothing about it. It was as if a mechanism inside of him had clicked—and that instant his career as a gambler was ended. This happened to him there in his room. He had no premonition of its being imminent and not enough curiosity to explore the fact afterward. That he had a fortune aside may or may not be a relevant consideration. It almost never happens that a gambler forsakes his passion because he has money enough. Money is not the thing.

My own opinion is that what clicked was his emotional apparatus. I mean that what had really occurred was a change of feeling toward the thing he had been doing. Whether he thought it right or wrong, he had come suddenly to dislike it. His heart could not be in it. In his remote self he was, and is, I think, a pagan,

with a kind of animistic religion that awakened in him
at his first contact with nature. Or perhaps it was
from Weaver he had got the idea that all things are
animated by a universal spirit.

This was at the beginning of the third year of the
World War. With that faculty of swift, unerring
imagination which may be mistaken for an occult
power and is no more rare than a free mind having
nothing preconceived, he saw two things clearly.

The war would go on for a long time yet, and the
price of wheat, which seemed already very high, would
continue to rise. It would rise to any fabulous price.
There was no telling. All that one had to do to win
was to buy it. He was so sure of this that he never
examined the conclusion. He could see it taking place.

Now looking back we may wonder why it was not
obvious to everyone. We almost forget that it was
not. We know for a fact that the wheat pit was
divided. Speculators were continually in a panic lest
the war should end overnight. Many stood obstinately
for a fall in wheat on the chance that it would. Anyhow, they said, wheat was already much too high to
buy for speculation. Which only shows, as Dreadwind
said, that the opportunity was such as gamblers dream
of and cannot imagine really. When it comes they will
not believe it. They are fettered by a sense of probability, whereas the great chance always presents itself
in the guise of extreme improbability. Their imagina-
tions were overwhelmed.

But think of it! At that time, though wheat seemed
very high, one who had started buying it and had

bought it steadily, blindly, without stopping to reflect, might have won a nabob's fortune. Capital was not necessary; only the vision to see and the nerve to go on, against every sense of probability. A mere shoe-string of capital, as little as fifty dollars, had been enough for one who knew how to parlay his bets—that is, to double progressively upon winnings. I stress this case a bit because it concerns also Weaver, as will appear. Weaver much more than Dreadwind.

Directly, in fact, it concerned Dreadwind little. Day after day he watched the price of wheat rise and never touched it. He had not the faintest inclination to do so. But it was a spectacle worth watching. He watched it with his mind, thoughtfully, attentively; his emotions were not involved. They were preoccupied in a way of their own. He was waiting. You may guess for what. For Cordelia, for spring, for the time when he should place himself across their path at that point of its annual beginning which he had located in tracing them backward.

Knowing the impetuosity of his nature you would think he fumed and rattled the calendar and stretched himself with idiotic anxieties. Not at all. Sitting there on the end of his spine with his feet in the window, idly regarding the tape as it passed through his fingers, he was serene and contented, in like manner with him who, having found the one pearl of great price, sold all that he had and bought it. That he did not physically possess the pearl was circumstantial. It existed. He had found it. He had surrendered everything to it. No violent lover's antics, which are never what they seem, but gestures of doubt, fear and irresolution. The form of his extravagance was tranquillity.

What we know at this time about the object is next to nothing. Put it all together. A glance or two from the woman across the hostility of a jealous father, a silent episode in the wheat field, a looking back, and then a token—the spikelet of wheat in flower—to be delivered to someone who might ask for her at the house from which she vanished. I'm sure he told it all, at least all that lay within the reach of words. It seems very little on which to found an ecstasy.

You may suppose the source of this ecstasy was the revelation of nature through which he had passed and that Cordelia was of this experience the passive symbol. Or you may suppose that the emotion of love is egoistic, having the subject within itself, requiring only that the object shall exist, wherefore the thought of it may be more exciting, more creative, than the reality. This would cause it to seem a thing not external to the man, not achieved in collaboration with him, but an edifice of his own imagination, corresponding to his power of abstract idealization. The object in that case is a myth.

But is there not always the possibility of a perfect instance? Is not the combined event of two coessential human beings the one great expectation? It may never yet have happened that we know of. Grant that it never has. Yet whence arises this expectation if the thing itself may not occur? I say no more. I merely add that if it happened accidentally, and yet of course in a predetermined way, there would be no intellectual

understanding of it.   Once it had recognized itself
nothing could alter it.   It would be as final as the fact
of one's birth.   Neither time nor space could touch it.
Never could it be less or more, nor could it ever be as
if it had not been.   A separation of its two principles
would be as impossible as self-division.   In that case—
I say, in that case, Dreadwind would not have worried
about when and how he should see Cordelia again.   He
had found her once for all.   And though he should
never see her again, still it would be the same—almost
the same.

However, be the case what it was, he sat for days
on end, running into winter, in a kind of waking dream,
while a tale went up and down La Salle Street about
an old wheat gambler who had gone mad with the rise.
The scene of his operations was the Open Board of
Brokers, and that institution was like a rickety net, set
close inshore for small and crippled fish, now about to
be wrecked by a whale.

The thing had been going on for some time before
anybody heard of it because nothing that happens on
the Open Board is properly noticeable.   The place itself is supposed to be invisible.   Yet no one can help
seeing it.   There it has stood for many years, with its
sign up, across the street from the great Chicago
Board of Trade.   It is one of the sights, only no one
who is respectable ever shows it to you or lets you go
there if he can help it.

If in passing with a member of the reputable Board
of Trade you ask what that is, he says, without looking
at it, "Oh, that's the Open Board."   Then if you ask

him what the Open Board is, he says, "It's something we can't get rid of." He may, if you press him, tell you how hard they did try to get rid of it. They couldn't because it was too deeply encysted in the community. So at last it was accepted, like the tainted relation it was, under an ambiguous treaty, which was that the Board of Trade would stop fighting it and blink at its existence if on its part it would undertake never to be seen or heard and to walk circumspectly in the twilight.

This treaty has been strictly observed. All the same, curiosity is stronger than respectability; and this was a very curious thing that had been going on. An old wheat gambler gone mad, one who never in his life had been right before and now apparently couldn't be wrong. Success is generally a positive test of sanity. This is different. There is no success in gambling really. There are only heights and depths. One who sets himself against chance, who defies it, who, so to say, wrings it by the beard and commands it to humor him, is a reckless fool. His moments of grandeur are in his mind and his belly will be kept with sops. But one who does this and wins—wins steadily, progressively, offensively—he must be mad. He is at least possessed. The gods are pleased to be ironic. They are mocking him. And such pleasantries have always some ghastly sequel. Other gamblers regard him with awe and fear. And such a thing will make talk wherever it happens.

Dreadwind first saw a paragraph about it in a newspaper column of wheat-pit gossip. Then an acquaintance whom he met in the street spoke of it lightly. This occurred a second and a third time, which was not strange, since everyone was beginning to wonder at it; and he asked for particulars. They were briefly stated. An old man who had been known for years on the Open Board as the unluckiest of bettors had all at once hit it right. Then it seemed he couldn't go wrong. Already he had run a few dollars into a fortune and was still going. It wasn't the amount of money people were thinking of; relatively that was not large, though of course—who knew?—it might at this rate, if his luck continued, exhaust all the gold in La Salle Street's bank vaults. No. What made the episode so humanly and irresistibly interesting was the setting. On the Open Board—that place!—among all those cripples and lepers of unluck, for one of them to rise like this, to be singled out for the great favor—well, it stirred the sentimental imagination of all that grim and haunted neighborhood.

"How does he trade?" Dreadwind asked.

"That's it," his informant answered. "He's been doing one thing all the time. He's been buying wheat. Nothing else. He's buying it still, as if he couldn't stop."

"Huh!" said Dreadwind. "A man needn't have been mad to do that."

Alone in his office, Dreadwind's thoughts kept returning to the subject. Someone had seen what he saw —that wheat was bound to go a great deal higher because the war would go on—and everyone thought him mad. An old derelict wheat gambler with a streak of clear vision at last and the courage to pursue it! He wondered what kind of old man that would be. He wondered also why he went on thinking about him.

He wasn't really interested beyond the simple fact. Still, there was all the time a feeling of effort in the back of his mind, as if it were trying to establish some very improbable association of ideas. Whatever that was, nothing came of it; instead, he was seized with an impulse to visit the Open Board and have a look for himself at the madman who had got his luck by the tail, as people thought, but who, as Dreadwind knew, had but the imagination to see an obvious thing.

He had passed the place often but he had never looked in.

It is a very large room, the size of a small theatre, on the street level. You walk right in, all the way in, and nobody asks you what you want or so much as gives you a look. I suppose that is why they call it the Open Board of Brokers. At the Board of Trade, as at the Stock Exchange, only members may go on the floor. Visitors are confined to the gallery. There is no gallery here. Brokers, customers and visitors are all together. It is a democratic arrangement, truly and naturally so, as everything is on the bottom plane. Nearly everyone here has already fallen and cannot fall any lower. The rest are such as cannot expect to rise. It was their plane to begin with.

On the Board of Trade the minimum quantity of phantom wheat one may buy or sell—the unit of trade —is five thousand bushels. Here one may trade in a hatful. It is petty gambling with the one merit of pretending to be nothing else. There are no cash tables, no samples of actual grain, no millers or millers' agents, nothing but prices to bet on; and these are not its own. They are received by wire from the big grain pits across the street.

At one end of the room, reaching to the ceiling, is a great blackboard, lighted from the top by an overhanging row of electric lamps. A kind of trestle board, six or seven feet from the floor, runs the whole length of the blackboard; and up and down this trestle board walks a man with a telephone receiver on a long cord fixed to his head, a bit of chalk in one hand and a piece of rag in the other. He receives in his ear the prices that originate on the Board of Trade across the way and chalks them up. When a column is full to the bottom he clears it with the rag and begins again at the top.

Under the blackboard is the trading pit—the round, hollow rostrum, twenty feet across, three steps up and three steps down. It is fiercely lighted by a circle of electric lamps hanging low from the ceiling. In the foreground facing it are some rows of wooden chairs such as you find in cheap theatres, screwed to the floor. A government weather map hanging to a post, a news ticker, telephone booths and sand boxes to spit in complete the equipment.

People are what you see. This cluster of humanity, in a place that would be dark as midnight at high noon if not for the artificial illumination, is in a state of constant working, not in the sense of performing labor but as a mass of separate organisms all entangled, apparently unaware of their contacts and mutual pressure, now one or two moving convulsively, then two or three more while those others are still, suddenly a violent spasm through the whole mass for no reason you can understand, then again a period of total inertia, with here and there a straggler prowling about. It makes one think of a body of worms—worms at the roots of the wheat—only that worms work silently. At least we cannot hear them. It is quite possible that they hear themselves and that what they hear is not unlike this low, raging sound to which the emotions of greed, envy, malice, disappointment and gloating contribute each its dissonance and which expresses the whole low motive. There is no uglier sound in the world. And it is inarticulate—that is to say, wordless. No intelligible words are heard. There are only shrieks, groans, jeers and jungle cries.

You will observe that these men have an affliction of the sight. They look at you, at each other, at moving objects, without seeing. Their gaze is inward except when it turns to the blackboard. What is written there they see, and almost nothing else.

How strange the gambling passion is! And how it levels men by making them oblivious of one another! Here you see one who might be a blacksmith, another who smells of the stockyards, men who keep their dignity in soiled linen, men whose wives are out washing, men who walk like rats, a few clean, well-kept old men for whom you feel a special distaste, and nearly everyone with some funny little tic or nervous habit— a way of pulling the nose or picking the fingers or step-

ping over cracks on the floor. A great proportion of
them are very old and long ago lost.

This was the scene on which Dreadwind entered.
With one glance he took it in. He understood it instantly in all institutional aspects. Yet he stood as one
petrified with astonishment.

There in the center of the pit, vividly marked out in
the light, stood Absalom Weaver. He stood alone
with a scornful, invincible air and had his back to the
blackboard. He did not need to see the prices. He
could téll how they changed by the reactions of those
who stood on the steps of the pit in a closed ring, facing him. They kept their eyes fixed upon him; he gazed
at the floor reflectively and moved his head slowly from
side to side with an air of listening. Just at that moment had come a lull in proceedings. The room was
still, everything having fallen into an eddy of silence as
may occur in the midst of a storm. The price of wheat
had not changed for some seconds, the chalk writer on
the trestle board was motionless, and minds were in a
state of tension.

But there was another unexpected object in that
room. In one bare corner of it, just inside the entrance
to the left, where the light was dim—there stood Cordelia. Like a splendid wheat stalk in a sty, thought
Dreadwind. He had a glimpse of her before he saw
Weaver. Having glanced at the pit scene he looked
at her again; and her face was averted. He was sure
she had seen him enter; she had been looking straight
at him. She was the only woman in the place, not
counting the one who kept the tobacco stand by the out-

side door; and no one was near her. As Dreadwind approached her he felt that she was aware of him. He stood at her side and still she did not look.

In that instant the price of wheat changed and the air of the room was blasted by a fury of sound. Dreadwind saw that she shuddered. He heard Weaver's voice above the tumult and looked toward the pit.

The old man was standing alone, still in the center of it. The howling ring seemed by some invisible means restrained from crowding in upon him. From the steps it leaned inward toward him, as far as possible, with its multiple neck stretched, with cries of rage, with flying arms and clawing fingers, as if but for that invisible restraint it would seize and tear him to pieces. But of course they were only selling wheat to him—phantom wheat. He was apparently the sole buyer. He bought it from them, bought all they dared sell, and then taunted them ——

"Farmers, are you through? Farmers of nonexistent acres, have you no more grain? A little more. I want it. Go sweep your bins and see. Ye who can reap what was never sown, surely you shall find a bushel more. You grow it in your minds. Come, grow me a little more."

The price changed again and his voice was drowned.

Dreadwind turned to look at Cordelia and found her regarding him with a sad, wondering expression. He realized that what he had just heard and seen was already old to her. She heard without hearing it; saw without seeing it; and hated it.

Not a word passed between them. He got some-

thing from his pocket and held it out to her in his
closed hand. She blushed a little, yet took it with no
hesitation or sign of surprise and put it away in her
dress, not looking to see what it was. Immediately he
left her.

Why? I did not ask him. It was his impulse. Undoubtedly he sensed the fact that she was humiliated
at his finding them in this vulgar environment.

What she had received from him in a little satin
case turned out to be an exact and exquisite reproduc-
tion, in jewels, precious metal and enamel, of that
wheat spikelet in flower he had once received from her
in an uninscribed envelope. With it was a slip of paper
bearing his address and telephone number. Nothing
else.

When he came the next day she was in the same
place. He went directly to her. She was wearing the
jewel at her throat. The first thing she did with a
naïve gesture was to hand him a slip of paper on which
their address was written. She had it ready and was
therefore expecting him.

"When may I come there?" he asked.

"We used to come from there straight here," she
said, "and go from here straight home again. Never
anywhere else. Lately on leaving here we've been
walking a good deal, just to go out of our way. That
takes a little time."

"To avoid the people who follow you?" he asked.

She nodded. "They're beginning to do that," she
said. "Father doesn't like it to be known where we
live."

"Why not a cab?" he asked.

"Yes," she said. "We tried that. But we had to keep giving the driver directions without knowing any place to go. It's better to walk."

Dreadwind was wondering how they lived—in what circumstances. The address was a number in Wabash Avenue, far down; it would be in the press of the city, where no one lived any more.

"We have some rooms there, over a store," she said, answering his thoughts. "Three. It's very simple."

She regarded him again with that wondering expression.

"What is it?" he asked.

For a moment she hesitated, then reddened and asked: "Do you do this too?"

By this she obviously meant what her father was doing over there in the pit. Did Dreadwind do a similar thing in another place? That was what she was asking.

"Once I did," he said. "Not any more." She seemed relieved and looked away; and he became distressed. "I think I know why your father does it," he added. "His reason is better than mine was."

This was delicate ground. First, his answer to her question implied a reflection on her father; then what he added in defence of him to mend that effect seemed clearly to imply that she had cast a reflection upon him to begin with.

"I was thinking of you," she said.

What he said next was utterly stupid. Still, it was the kind of stupidity that does not matter.

"Did you know I tried all summer to find you?" he asked.

She looked at him gravely for a moment, the trace of a smile appeared, and she made no answer.

CHAPTER IX

T HAT evening Dreadwind called.

Their rooms were on the top floor of one of those very old brick-wall buildings that have still enough economic life left to pay taxes while the land continues to increase in value for the steel structures that will ultimately dispossess them. The entrance lay between haberdashery and musical instruments. The character of the tenantry above was indicated by tin signs and placards on the walls of the hallway and on the stair risers—a painless dental parlor, a manufacturer of sporting novelties, a banjo teacher, a job printer, Prof. Ranjit, presumably a vender of bottled darkness, and so on. At the top of each stairway was a low-burning gas jet. The place was very still. The uppermost floor, which was the fourth, had the appearance of being unoccupied until Dreadwind saw far back a light showing through a transom. There he knocked.

The response was not immediate. After several moments of silence light footsteps approached the door. The bolt clicked and Cordelia looked out. Seeing who it was she opened the door wide and said good evening.

What Dreadwind entered was evidently their

kitchen, dining room and living room all in one. It was lighted by gas, burning in a single jet at the end of a pipe that came straight down from the ceiling and terminated in a snakish curve. A black iron sink in one corner. Some pieces of crockery on a painted shelf. On a box by the window a one-burner gas stove, the flame at low duty under a kettle of water. On the window ledge outside milk bottles and food parcels. That was the larder. They had just dined on milk, bread, cheese and stewed prunes. The things had not been cleared off the table, which was covered with checkered oilcloth. Two wooden chairs were a little pushed back from it. The walls were decorated in a startling way with three-color advertising posters, fine half-tone impressions in black and white, and innumerable miscellany of the printing art—pasted to the wall with no thought of symmetry, order or agreement. Once this had been a job pressroom. There was an odor of printer's ink, chemicals, strange incense, dried paste and closed plumbing.

Under the gas light in a folding canvas chair sat Weaver. A dish of coffee was on the floor beside him. His knees were as high as his face. Open on one knee, as it were a pulpit-stand, lay the book he was reading —Paracelsus Theophrastus Bombastus in Latin.

"Even to his habitation will ye seek and come," he said, looking at Dreadwind. That was his salutation.

"I have an errand with you," said Dreadwind.

"He has an errand," the old man retorted. "No doubt he has an errand. That which is smoke is the mercurial principle. That which burns is the sulphurous principle. What remains is the ash." He was so pleased with this delphic saying that he remembered the uses of hospitality. "Will you break bread with us?" he asked.

Cordelia gave Dreadwind an expectant look and stood poised, with an arm already reached out toward the things she would prepare if he should say yes.

"Another time, if you will ask me," he said.

"Some coffee, then. Bring him a dish of coffee, ye mercurial principle."

She moved to do this; but Dreadwind declined again.

"My errand is with you alone," he said to Weaver.

"Leave us, Cordelia," said the old man.

He put his book face down on his knee, brought his ten finger tips together and gazed over them fixedly at Dreadwind, who, when Cordelia was gone, sat on one of the wooden chairs, facing him.

"So you are the evil spirit one hears of in the wheat fields," said Dreadwind in a low tone. "Father Rust himself. The killer of wheat."

There was a hardening of Weaver's expression from a change in his eyes; nothing else. He did not move, but continued to gaze steadily at his acuser.

"That bag you dropped the morning I surprised you by the roadside—I know what was in it," said Dreadwind. "The seed of rust. Enough to have killed half the wheat in Kansas."

The old man's eyes did not flinch.

"I might deliver you to the law," said Dreadwind, and waited.

"You might," said Weaver thoughtfully. "You might do that very thing. If it worries thee thou shouldst."

"I don't intend to," said Dreadwind.

"I know you don't intend to," said Weaver.

"However," said Dreadwind, "I'm not the only person who knows what you've been sowing on the wind. I couldn't have found out without letting others know. I mean that no matter what I intend to do the law may find you out."

"It may," said the old man. "That is quite possible. Even so."

His voice was calm, quite level, with a note of taunting in it. Dreadwind was baffled. He regarded the old man with wonder. Could he be blind to the enormity of his offense? Was he a monster then? Or had he in him some deformed, fanatical conviction by which he justified his acts? In any respect, what a fatalist he was!

"You must see the implications," said Dreadwind. "They are damning. In one personality you go about the country casting death upon the wheat, pretending all the time to love and cherish it. In another personality you are a gambler in Chicago betting on the price to rise. First, you destroy the food itself; then you seek to profit by that wickedness. The more you kill with rust the scarcer wheat will be and the higher it will rise. That's how any jury on earth would see it. I can't help seeing it that way myself."

There it was all naked. They looked at each other for a whole minute. Then in a low tone Weaver said:

"Pretend is a strong word. A heinous word. I cannot forgive it."

That one word he seized upon. Evidently nothing else in the accusation had hurt at all.

"You have been doing this now for a long time," said Dreadwind, as if he knew it. There was no denial. "For years," he added. Still no sign or gesture of denial. He continued relentlessly. "Each year the new wheat runs to meet you. Do you remember? Silly wheat! How easily you deceive it! Or perhaps it cannot imagine treachery. Is that it? And yet it knows. When you come with your sack of plague it knows. I saw that too. I saw it turn and run from you in terror."

He had touched the thing at last.

With a singular continuous effort Weaver rose. For a moment he stood poised in a menacing attitude, looking down at Dreadwind. Then he put his hands behind him and began to walk, in a blind, trampling way, precisely as he had walked through the wheat that morning. The chair capsized and was propelled aside as if it were invisible and without weight. His book was trodden underfoot. The dish of coffee overturned and he did not see it. These sounds brought Cordelia to the door. He did not see her, either. She stood looking from one to the other with a curious, unfrightened expression. Dreadwind now was standing. Suddenly the old man stopped and faced him.

"What will you have of me?" he asked.

"Your reasons," said Dreadwind.

"You spoke of the farmers," said Weaver.

"I did not," said Dreadwind.

"You said they would hang me."

"I did not," said Dreadwind.

"You said what was true.   They would," said
Weaver. "They would hang me with a hempen rope.
But they hang themselves, they hang each other, with
a rope they cannot see, a rope that does not exist. It's
name is surplus. Reasons—what? Reasons? There
is only one. I did not make it. Nor do I understand
it. Tell me if you do. Tell me why less brings more
than plenty. Why do seven bushels profit the farmer
more than ten? If you know why that is then everything else is clear. You don't know. Nobody knows.
And why will the farmer grow ten instead of seven?
The surplus, what is called the surplus—the rope that
hangs him—it is in the last three bushels. Yet he will
produce them. He cannot help it. He must keep that
bargain I spoke of—his side of it—which is to defend
wheat from its enemies and give it space; and wheat
in its boundless gratitude hath overwhelmed him. Now
what? Shall the farmer who produces plenty be destroyed by his own industry? Or ———"

He paused, gazing all the time at Dreadwind, and
when he spoke again his voice was altered.

"The wheat," he said. "The wheat itself. You
spoke of that."

"I did," said Dreadwind. "I spoke of that."

"That I stretched forth my hand against it."

"Yes," said Dreadwind.

"Thou didst," said Weaver, extending his arm and
pointing his finger. At a certain intensity of personal

feeling he went naturally to the archaic pronouns and his tones became sepulchral. Does it sound theatrical? But it was effective because the emotion required that mode of expression. "Abominably thou didst," he continued. "And that of all things was the one thou shouldst not have spoken of—to me. I say again, if it troubles thee in thy mind thou shouldst tell it to the law. Sooner do that than speak of it again—to me."

That was his period. It required an exit. There was always the possibility that he consciously dramatized such moments; but even if he did there was never anything false about the action. It expressed the deep and permanent phantasy of his being. That one has invented one's own phantasy does not stultify the acting of it provided the invention to begin with was true to one's nature. Weaver's was. He lived a made-up tragedy, acted a self-assigned rôle, and yet it was all true.

Having made the period he groped his way to the door through imaginary darkness—toward the outer door through which Dreadwind had entered, the door in which Cordelia was standing. She moved to let him pass, turning her back to the jamb. For a while he paced the hallway, Cordelia watching him from the doorway. His steps gradually diminished. Then a door opened and closed and all was still. He had gone into his room, which opened off the hall separately, as all the rooms did.

With a glance at Dreadwind, Cordelia disappeared. He heard the same door open and close again. She was gone for perhaps fifteen minutes; and when she returned she made coffee and placed it before him in a yellow bowl, together with bread in the whole loaf and a large segment of cheese. He was to help himself. She did this all without speaking, as if she had done it before. Then she sat down at the end of the table and regarded him in a slow, musing manner, with no guise of defense or shyness.

"Will anything happen?" she asked.

"From what you heard us talking about just now?" She nodded.

"No," he answered. "I don't think so. Do you remember I said I believed your father's motive was better than mine had been? That was when you asked me, there by the wheat pit, if I did that too."

"I remember," she said.

"Well, I'm sure of it now," he said. "Shall I tell you why?"

She shook her head. "A woman to her own understanding," she said. "He taught me that," she added with a sober smile.

"Your father is not looking so well," said Dreadwind.

"He never does here," she said. "And this time it's worse with him. You see, always before he has lost— in the first week or ten days everything there was, only just enough to keep us through the winter. That made the winters very long for him. But this is different. Now he is winning. He doesn't tell me. But I know it."

"It doesn't change your way of living," said Dreadwind.

"No," she said. "It isn't that. We should not know how to live in any other way. He is different. I hardly know him."

"How has he changed?" Dreadwind asked. "Does he talk of getting rich?"

"Rich?" she repeated. It was a strange word. "No," she said, "I'm sure he never thinks of that. It's something he will do to wheat. In the night he thinks he is still there—in that dreadful place—calling for wheat—buying it higher and higher ——" She stopped her ears. "Then something happens. I don't know what that is. He is breathless for a moment and then he cries, 'Ten dollars a bushel for all you've got!' Do you understand it?"

"It comes together," he said. "Yes, I think I do."

They talked like this for hours. The fact of themselves they took for granted in some extraordinary sense that neither of them paused to consider. They asked and answered questions in an artless, unreserved manner, exactly as if all these things had happened to them during a long separation.

She told him of her life with Weaver from the beginning, with apparently no thought of how preposterous the pattern of it was. Initio, that early winter night when she ran out of the door after him with her arctics flapping, a child of ten. He did not hear her; when she caught him by the coat, he picked her up, kissed her, set her down again and turned away, walking faster than before. She was puzzled for a moment and very desolate. She had made her choice. Everything in her little world she had cast away to follow him and apparently he did not want her.

She looked back at the house. Someone had closed the door. No one was calling. The light burned brightly in the kitchen window, as if nothing had happened. How often it had beckoned her home, saying, "Hurry! Hurry! Nothing will catch you, but do hurry!" And now it seemed not to know her. It had cut her off; and the house was strange. It did not occur to her to go back. She ran after her father again, a terror of loneliness clutching her heart. Overtaking him a second time she put her hand in his. He neither spoke nor looked at her; but she knew he wanted her; and thus they walked a long way without resting. For many days they walked when it was not too cold; when it was they lodged with strangers who treated them with aloof curiosity and called her little girl. Then they stopped for the winter at a place where he taught a country school.

In the spring they set out again, walking south to meet the harvest. This was the beginning of a tryst which they kept annually thereafter. In Texas they faced about and followed the sickle bar all the way to the Red River of the North. He worked as a harvest hand. She was too small to do anything. He took her education in hand. She could already read and write; but they had only two books. One was that volume of Paracelsus, the other was a small Bible; and these were of equal value. More had been luggage; and it was their way to live without impedimenta of any sort. There was never anything to carry. The clothes they wore and what they had in their pockets—that was all. At any moment they were free to rise and go.

He taught her in the rabbinical manner, through her ears. This method had notable merits. Classes had neither time nor place, no beginning and no end. They were continuous, opportune and always interesting. You got your Latin verbs with whatever it was you were doing, astronomy on starry nights, history on rainy days, literature to relieve the tedium of a day's journey; botany, biology, chemistry and physics where and however the true phenomenon occurred in nature's laboratory. Everything was explained as it happened and then related to all that was known before. And just as one began to think the garden of knowledge had been explored, then suddenly new vistas were opened, extending to the mysteries. He had been himself trained for the church and had, besides, a fine gift for teaching. Surely never before had a woman been so educated, and wholly to a man's liking. Of the things women teach each other she knew very little, for she had few friendships and no intimacies among members of her own sex. And of the things a lover teaches she knew nothing at all.

So passed the three enchanted seasons—spring, summer, autumn—in a state of idyllic vagabondage. But the winter was a horrible nightmare. Then her world fell to pieces.

At first she did not understand why they came to the city in the wintertime. They lived in one room and she kept house on tiptoe. He would leave each morning shortly before nine and return at three; and if she was lonesome while he was absent, with no one to talk to and so much to be afraid of, it was even worse when he was there, though of course in another way. Their companionship ceased. He was gloomy, preoccupied, often ironic and irritable. She did not know what he did and could not bring herself to ask. She hardly dared, and besides, she dreaded to find out.

Still, one day she followed him to where he suddenly disappeared through a large doorway. She waited a long time and then, as he did not come out and as many people were continually passing both ways through the doorway, she thought perhaps it was some kind of thoroughfare and ventured far enough in to hear the wicked uproar that rises from the wheat pit—from any wheat pit, but especially from the one at the Open Board of Brokers.

She was terrified. Her first impulse was to rush in and find him and beg him to come away with her— back to their beautiful country where nothing like this could ever be. Instead, she ran all the way back to their room and crouched there until he returned. He noticed how strange she was and questioned her anxiously, but she avoided telling him what she had done.

That evening he was much more himself. The next morning he took her with him and left her with the woman at the tobacco stand just inside the door. Every day thereafter he took her with him. That was how it started; and now she went with him because he needed her. She would be afraid to let him go by himself, he was so unseeing, so unpresent among realities. She doubted whether he knew where they lived or could find his way home alone. He had long leaned upon her figuratively; now he was beginning to lean upon her actually, as they walked. That was only here, in the city, and more now than ever before. In the country he walked in his own strength.

And this for all these years had been the design of their lives together. The winters, ah, yes. They were not to be remembered. But always came spring again and with it the delightful wandering, with happiness running in their footsteps. They came to have a regular orbit. And as Weaver grew to be known among the people therein he worked less and less as a harvest hand until he ceased to do so at all, and became as one of the ancient magi, a man full of arts and knowledge, giving shrewd and profitable counsel to the wise, performing offices of sorcery for the superstitious, thus gradually assuming the character in which Dreadwind found him.

In a few years also Cordelia became helpful. She filled her apron in the harvest. Between them they gained a livelihood easily, and came each winter to Chicago with enough money to keep them in the way they were wont to subsist, and the moiety over that Weaver lost in the wheat pit.

"Last times make one a little sad," she said. "Not that one would wish to go on and on forever. Only because it is the last time. I wonder why."

"What was for the last time?" he asked.

"All the beautiful part," she said. "That harvest was our last. Only the winter is left. I can't see what will happen. Perhaps I don't wish to see."

"When did you begin to have this feeling?" he asked. "Suddenly, just now? Or has it been growing?"

"To everything we knew I said good-bye this year," she answered.

"Places," he said.

She nodded. "Places. Friendly things. Bits of scenery. Trees we had named and treated as people. A little church with a graveyard we came to one night in a dreadful storm. We saw it far off by the lightning and ran. The door was unlocked. We were there until morning. It was the first summer; and there he christened me Cordelia."

"That was not the name you started with?"

"No. There in the church, with the thunder splitting itself on the steeple, he read King Lear to me. From memory, I mean. He knew it by heart. The church was dark. His voice filled it and echoed round. By the lightning flashes I could see him walking up and down the aisle. Then I knelt at the altar and he christened me Cordelia. Things like that," she concluded.

"And a bench," he wondered. "A certain round bench under an apple tree."

She blushed; looking at him steadily. "That was not good-bye," she said, "and Mrs. Purdy ought not to have told you."

No more than that did they say of the affair of their hearts. I had almost said no nearer than that did they come to it. But it had no external relation. It existed like a third part of them. It was the fact implicit; ex-

plicit facts merely pertained to it. And so also with
the fulfillment. That was to be long postponed and
it did not matter. It was never their way to make
words of their love.

Dreadwind was of Cordelia's notion that Absalom
Weaver's orbit was broken. More than this, he had
a sense of impending disaster. That was not surpris-
ing with the shape of facts in view. People thought
Weaver was running on luck. Dreadwind knew better.
The old man had got a gambling position in wheat
that was fundamentally logical. He would undoubtedly
push it to the last extreme. There was no foretelling
the sequel. There was only the probability that it
would be catastrophic. On reflection this seemed in-
evitable. There was no way of stopping him. Fear,
self-interest, satiety, a sense of consequences to himself
and others—such constraining modes of thought and
feeling were lacking in him. He had a demonic end
in view. He cared nothing for the temple. He denounced it. One could imagine that he wished to
destroy it. To what might follow he was utterly
indifferent.

The spectacle fascinated Dreadwind. With rapid
strokes of imagination he gave it form and projection.
It had an unpredictable dimension. In a game itself
without limits a fanatic who knew no restraint had got
the fatal hand. What if he should play it out? And
there was no reason to suppose he would not. Only
one of Dreadwind's prescience would have sensed the
possibilities. It is a fact that no one else did. How
could the keepers of the great world wheat market

have been attending properly to their business and watching at the same time for a mad comet to burst from the door of that mean little place across the street —the Open Board of Brokers—where nothing of primary importance could ever happen?

Afterward for a long time, you may remember, nobody quite believed it as it really was. Many thought Dreadwind was behind Weaver, had invested money in him, and was himself the daring principal. Circumstances gave some fictitious color to this belief, and as it was never denied by anyone who positively knew the truth it still persists in legend.

Dreadwind did of course stand by, for a reason that now comes clear. A romantic reason, you see. He could not avert the catastrophe. It would not have occurred to him to try. Cordelia was his true anxiety.

His way of standing by was literal. He took all the rooms across the hall, furnished them in one day, and moved in.

Weaver apparently was never consciously aware of this astonishing gesture. At least he never spoke of it. A good deal of the time he seemed insensible to his surroundings and what passed therein; or, waking to them suddenly, he either accepted them indifferently or treated them as having been long familiar.

In that way he accepted Dreadwind without question or curiosity. Cordelia got another wooden chair and made a third place at the end of the table. Weaver said nothing. Dreadwind came every evening and ate with them. Weaver sometimes spoke when the guest arrived and sometimes gave him no recognition other than to include him tacitly. Afterward he would sit under the gas jet, in his folding chair, with his dish of coffee on the floor, and read while Cordelia cleared the table, Dreadwind contentedly watching her. He would go on reading while they walked in the hall and sometimes he passed them silently on the way to his room.

Then one evening it pleased him to talk. A fly fell into his bowl of milk. He fished it out, dried its feet, sent it away, and a flood of discourse fell from him, beginning with the fly as a marvelous instance and dwelling at length upon the enigma of becoming and being in all things. He talked for an hour continuously. He was on his feet, looking at them, with a thought half out of his mind, when of a sudden his interest broke. He forgot what he had been saying, looked once or twice around, then turned abruptly and went to his room.

Not long after this Dreadwind one evening had dinner sent in from his rooms. Weaver sat perfectly still until the Japanese man had placed it on the table and was gone, under Dreadwind's instructions not to remain to serve it.

"Would we had died by the hand of the Lord in the land of Egypt when we sat by the fleshpots," said Weaver; and asked for his bread and milk. Seeing they did not eat he added gently: "Empty sayings nourish old age. I am too fond of them. But all things are good, so ye eat not of darkness. Partake and mind not the lion who cheweth straw."

But they never did it again.

There was no fault in his faculties. He became each

day a little more unseeing, more indifferent to what
went on around him, and his feet grew heavy and reluctant; but when he entered the pit his bodily vigor
returned to him as from a draught of magic elixir; he
recovered his full stature and with it his aggressive,
saturnine manner; his mind was alert, sensitive and
unerring.   There his strength was.   He used it up
prodigally, exultingly, wasted it in excessive humors.
And his power increased.   He made no mistakes.
Dreadwind and Cordelia watched him in silent wonder.

One day as they stood together in a corner of the
room, looking on, a strange note rose out of the pit.
It was nearly time for gambling to cease.   Someone
had called Weaver by name.   Cordelia started.   Then
others began calling him by name, and presently many
were intoning it rhythmically.   The sound was boister-
ous and friendly, and one would have thought they
were proud of him.

"What does it mean?" Cordelia asked.

"It's a send-off," said Dreadwind.

"Why that?" she asked.

"I've been on the point of telling you ever since I
came in.   I heard it outside and came around at once.
This is his last day here.   He has bought a member-
ship on the Board of Trade.   I suppose that was never
heard of before—a man going to the Board of Trade
from this place.   And they are all a little excited about
it."

"He will go to the big wheat pit across the street—
is that what you mean?" said Cordelia.

Dreadwind nodded.   The closing gong had just

sounded and they were giving the old man a regular hazing. All the reserve with which his manner had inspired them was broken down, now that he was leaving. They dragged him out of the pit, pulled his hat over his ears, tied his muffler in three hard knots, rumpled his garments, beat him, jostled him, and then all with one impulse they picked him up and carried him toward the door, cheering and shouting his name. He took it passively. Cordelia and Dreadwind rescued him at last. He walked off between them and never looked back.

One who had taken no part in the hazing and resembled a huge wading fowl stood in the doorway croaking: "He will be back. . . . He will be back." Dreadwind looked at Cordelia to see if she heard. She was shaking her head.

That evening Dreadwind referred to the change. "May I introduce you to the wheat pit?" he asked.

"I washed my steps in butter and the rock poured me forth oil," Weaver answered. From which Dreadwind understood that he wished to find his way alone.

He made his first appearance the next morning. Cordelia and Dreadwind watched from the gallery. He stood on the edge of the wheat pit and did nothing. Nobody noticed him overtly, and that was a kind of hazing. Generally a new member is tumbled about a bit just to develop the nature of his goat. Everyone knew who he was of course and eyed him surreptitiously. For three days he stood there on the edge of the maelstrom, doing nothing.

And it was a maelstrom really. Wheat was two dollars and fifty cents a bushel, and still rising.

Who dared to buy wheat at this great price?

None of the little gamblers. They were afraid. They sold it rather—sold it because they were afraid.

None of the big gamblers were buying it, either. They, too, were afraid, though for a different reason. The rise in the price of wheat was beginning to have an ominous social aspect. A public cry had been raised against the pit. It was widely believed that the principal Chicago gamblers, having bought the crop at much lower prices from the farmers, were now turning it into gold at the expense of the countries allied against Germany in a war which was about to become our war as well. This was wicked in itself and very repugnant to our sympathies; but at the same time the American bread eater was mulcted in a like manner. So the public believed. And it had been true. But all the big, respectable gamblers were now standing aside, fearful of an experience in the pillory of public opinion if the Government should act suddenly and catch them red-handed in the business of profiteering.

And yet the price of wheat kept rising. Who bought it? Who was the reckless customer that went on buying it, regardless of the price of political consequences. Answer: WAR.

War was that kind of customer. Price was no object. The agents of France and Great Britain added each day millions of bushels to what the wheat pit called "that Eastern account." The orders originated in New York, where the Allied Buying Commission sat.

But do you remember? This pit stuff is phantom wheat. Armies do not subsist upon imaginary food. Why did they buy that?

For this reason: That to a certain extent and under certain conditions phantom wheat bought in the pit may be converted into actual grain on the railroad track. If the seller of phantom wheat cannot, when called upon, deliver the actual grain he must settle in cash. So the buyer will get either the wheat itself or a profit in money. The Allied Commission was buying both phantom wheat and actual grain at the same time. This is to be remembered. It was running a corner such as had never been dreamed of in the world before —a corner in wheat at Chicago with the Bank of England behind it.

There was yet one other heedless buyer.

On the fourth day Weaver went one step down into the pit and began to buy. On the fifth day he went another step down, still buying. On the sixth day he stood in the center and bought heavily. That was his regular place thereafter; and it came to be that he had a clear space around him, at the very core of the swirl, as it had been in the little wheat pit across the street, a figure for the eye to dwell upon. It came also that he was treated with awe and foreboding, like an event with no place in the probability of things.

Never here, as in that other pit, did he taunt the sellers or appear exulting. Why this was nobody knew. He was grim and silent. He would stand for sometimes an hour, motionless, gazing at the floor, at a distant object, or at Cordelia sitting always in the gallery with her regard upon him. Then of a sudden, with a sweeping look at the faces in the howling ring above him, he would lift his hands in signal and take all of that weighless, impalpable wheat they were willing to hurl down at him. No one ever saw him make a selling gesture. He never sold. And his profits were running wild, for the price knew not how to fall. Always he bought. Always it rose.

A few weeks after Weaver's advent on the Board of Trade America put her fist in the war.

The price of wheat was then approaching three dollars a bushel. The public cry against the pit increased, and not without reason in morals, for of course if gamblers were manipulating the price of wheat for private greed that now was both unpatriotic and abominable. Dreadwind spoke to Weaver. How could he reconcile what he was doing with any sense of common duty? The old man took thought and answered slowly:

"The pit cannot grow one blade of grass. Neither can it destroy one grain of wheat. There is so much wheat. No more, no less. It is only the price."

"But what of profiteering?" Dreadwind asked.

"So," said Weaver. "What of it? Tell me of it. I have seen war before. I know what it's lined and stuffed with. For once . . . you shall see . . . this time, I say . . . the spoils of war shall gild the wheat and nothing else. This is justice and I am its instrument. Its path shall be as a shining light."

Came now the month of May. All the gambling was in May wheat. And on the eleventh day, which was Friday, the price touched three dollars and a quarter a bushel!

Minds were tense with dread. Men could not say what it was they dreaded; but something was about to happen. It was written in the air. The emeritus honorable J. P., guardian elephant of the wheat pit, walked round and round it saying, exhortively: "Boys, don't touch it. For everybody's sake let that May wheat alone."

And there in the center stood Weaver, from time to time lifting his hands and taking all the wheat above him. Almost no gambler would touch wheat to buy it. Many were still willing to sell it.

That was the day the two British members of the Allied Buying Commission who had been buying wheat with the Bank of England behind them arrived in Chicago to look things over.

I happened myself to know the illuminating particulars. Dreadwind did not. He knew only the outcome; I told him what is here to be set down.

This is what happened: When J. P. with his head wagging returned to his desk from walking round and round the wheat pit his telephone was ringing. The two British members of the Allied Buying Commission were invited to lunch at the Union League Club. Would J. P. come? Yes, he would come, he said, on two conditions. One was that the Federal District Attorney should be asked; the other was that he himself should be permitted to speak. Both conditions were accepted.

At the lunch, besides the two English wheat buyers,

the Federal District Attorney and J. P., were seated all the great men of La Salle Street and all the lords of speculation in meat products and breadstuffs, including the bankers who kept unlimited credit at the disposal of Moberly's Dearborn Grain Corporation, who owned it in fact, but who would not suffer themselves to be called speculators. Anything else.

When the amenities were amiably exhausted J. P. rose.

"I want the Federal District Attorney to listen to this," he said. "Wheat is three dollars and a quarter a bushel and going up. For this we are damned. The Board of Trade is damned. I am damned. Most of the eminent gentlemen sitting here are damned. Now I want to ask a few questions. You"—he pointed to the financier who was chairman of Moberly's Dearborn Grain Corporation, calling his name—"have you got any May wheat?" The answer was no. One by one he called them, each in his name, and asked the same question, exhorting the Federal District Attorney to listen. The answer was invariably no. None of the great men of La Salle Street, none of the lords of speculation in meat products and breadstuffs, had any May wheat. They could not produce among them one kernel of it. "Now I ask myself," said J. P., "I ask myself the same question. 'Have you got any May wheat, J. P.?' On my word I answer, 'No, not a bushel.' Now wait. I'm not through. I ask our English visitors, 'Are you buying May wheat in the Chicago pit at this price?'"

They denied it.

"Be that as it may," said J. P. "I don't believe all
I hear. Just now as I was passing the pit a man took
me aside to say he had bought another lot of May
wheat for that Eastern account. Be that as it may—
. . . What's that?"

The English visitors interrupted him to say that if
what he had heard were true it was merely the tail-end
of some buying that had been ordered many days
before.

"Be that as it may," said J. P. again. "We haven't
come to the question yet. The question is: How much
May wheat have you got?"

The Englishmen conferred aside and decided to
react bluntly. They announced that they had nearly
thirty millions of bushels.

"That's as I thought it was," said J. P. "Now then,
I ask you all, what are we going to do? These gentlemen on their wheat-pit contracts are entitled to receive
at the end of this month thirty million bushels of wheat
in Chicago. Where is that wheat? The elevators are
empty. We have only a handful or two. We cannot
deliver this wheat. Why? Because it does not exist.
If these gentlemen insist and we cannot deliver the
wheat we shall have to pay them eight, nine, maybe
ten dollars a bushel, anything they say, to let us off.
We are sleeping on dynamite. Unless we can think
of something to do we shall be blown up. The Board
of Trade will blow up."

It was the truth of arithmetic, and so very simple
that no one realized it until J. P. had stated it in his
naïve way. The great men of La Salle Street and the

lords of speculation were dazed. The English buyers, with the Bank of England behind them were politely sympathetic. What could they do? They had not been acting as individuals. They had nothing to win or lose. They had been buying wheat for the Allies. They wanted the wheat. If the people they had bought it from were unable to deliver it—well, that would be rather awkward, wouldn't it? Yes, quite. That was to say, they had the wheat pit by what it sneezed with. When they were through there would be no wheat gamblers left in Chicago. Yes, one. His name would be Weaver.

But all the time the guardian elephant had a wicked light in his eye. He gathered together the great men of La Salle Street and all the lords of speculation in meat products and breadstuff, locked them into a room, and kept asking them one question: What were they going to do to save themselves? All the next day, which was Saturday, and all of the next, which was Sunday, they faced it; and they came at last, reluctantly, to the only answer there was.

They would shut the pit to May wheat. And anyone who had sold phantom wheat for May delivery and was unable on demand to produce it should be let off at a price to be determined by a special committee.

This had never been done before. In all the days of the Board of Trade, through panics and corners, it had never been done. Yet there was nothing else to do. "Unless you shut up," said J. P., "you will blow up." And that was true.

Dreadwind heard of this action before it was published. He had been anxiously watching. After dinner Sunday evening he said to Cordelia: "Be not surprised at anything tomorrow."

"Can you tell me?" she asked.

"I can tell you what will happen on the Board of Trade," he said. "Nothing. A notice will be posted on the bulletin board. And that is what it will say. Nothing shall happen. How this will affect your father I cannot imagine."

Five minutes before the opening of the pit on Monday morning Dreadwind joined Cordelia in the Board of Trade gallery. "I almost think it had been better to tell him," he said. "There is still time."

"No, wait," she said.

They had decided the night before to let the event weave it own pattern.

At first there was apparently nothing strange in the scene below them. But as the minutes passed—one, two, three—anyone who knew how an excited wheat market should come open must have been extremely oblivious not to notice how wrong the omens were. Where were those with glinting eyes and tautened nerves who should now be massed within the pit, gathered on the rim of it, overflowing all around, ready at the sound of a gong to rip the air apart with sound? Where were those who should be running to and fro between the pit and every other point, bringing news and last instructions? One minute yet until the opening and the pit was hardly one-third full. The men already gathered were not tense and poised; they were dilatory and apathetic. They stood in little groups

talking together.   And on the dial above the pit where
price changes are recorded was the sign of September wheat—S E P.   Where was the sign of M A Y?
Nobody was interested in September wheat.   All the
gambling was in May wheat.   The great corner with
the Bank of England behind it and Absalom Weaver
astride of it was in May wheat.

And the sign of May had disappeared!

None of this had Weaver noticed.   Both his mind
and his eyes were in distant focus.   He stood in his
place at the center of the pit.   Once he glanced uneasily
at the clock and then at the thin fringe of men around
him.   Still he was not warned.

The gong struck.

CHAPTER X

NO blast of sound assailed the ear. It was as if a cannon had missed fire. Here and there a voice was heard naming September wheat. May was not named at all. Most of those ranged round the pit stood at ease, idly looking on.

"May! May!" called Weaver, with now an alarmed and dazed expression.

There was a moment of stillness. Then a voice said: "Go read what's on the board. There's no such thing as May wheat."

Weaver heard. He walked out of the pit to the bulletin board. There stood the notice of his defeat. He read:

At a special meeting of the directors of the Chicago Board of Trade it was decided to discontinue trading in May wheat. All existing contracts shall be adjusted either by delivery of the property—the actual wheat—or at the settling price to be determined by a special committee to be appointed by the president of the Board. Patriotic duty to the country in this hour of national stress prompted the directors in reaching their conclusion to take this unprecedented action.

(Signed) BY THE PRESIDENT OF THE BOARD.

Thus the wheat pit was saved. Thus all the gamblers who had sold phantom wheat which they could not deliver were saved. They would be able to settle at a reasonable price, at a price to be determined by themselves. And the greatest wheat corner in all time, the only one that ever had the Bank of England behind it, was beaten by the simple expedient of shutting up the gambling layout.

Weaver stood there before the notice for a long time, motionless, with a fixed expression. Then he turned and walked slowly back to the pit. Standing again at the center of it he held up both hands, all fingers extended, the palms toward himself. This is the buying gesture. Each finger and thumb calls for five thousand bushels. He shouted:

"May wheat! . . . May wheat! . . . Is this a wheat market? . . . I'll buy May wheat at three-fifty."

There was no response. The ring stared at him in embarrassment, not knowing how to act.

"At four dollars!" he shouted.

His voice filled that enormous room. All other sound had ceased. The wheat pit now began to fill up with spectators drawn from the corn pit, the cash tables and elsewhere.

"Five!" he shouted.

Voices were lifted against him. Angry voices, saying: "You're breaking the rules!" "Expel him!" "Bughouse!" "Get the committee!" "Who do you think you are?"

Several approached, meaning evidently to dissuade him gently. He thrust them aside.

"Six," he shouted. "Six dollars a bushel for May wheat! Eight! Nine! I call you to witness I am bidding nine dollar a bushel for May wheat! Mark it up there. May wheat is nine dollars. Put it up."

Many were now turning away, some with expressions of disgust, others with morbid faces. He wheeled once all around, sustaining the buying gesture of the extended fingers and inturned palms, and shouted for the last time:

"*Ten!* I bid ten dollars a bushel for May wheat. All you've got."

A committee arrived. Four men pushed their way authoritatively into the pit and surrounded Weaver. He did not resist, for he was through. They led him out of the pit. On the top step his feet stumbled and almost he had fallen; but they held him up and brought him to the gate where Cordelia and Dreadwind were waiting. One of the four whispered to Dreadwind: "Get him home. Keep him away from here. His lamp is out."

Cordelia walked on one side of him and Dreadwind on the other, anxiously; he declined support from either of them. When they were outside Dreadwind signaled for a cab. The old man shook his head, pulled away from them and plunged alone into the traffic. From his manner it was evident he had a destination and an errand both. They caught up with him and walked as before, one on each side, a little surprised that he knew his own way and wondering at his air of purpose.

At the door of the La Salle Hotel he turned in.

There in the big ballroom several hundred farmers were assembled. They represented a national grain

growers' association, by whatever the latest name was
for that chronic futility. The name is changed every
little while. There is no other way to renew the delusion that farming is a business, to sustain the hope that
ultimately the producers of food, like the organized
producers of all fabricated and glittering things, shall
be able to say what they will take and how much they
will give. But by any name it is always the same
thing. This was the annual convention. The subject
was coöperative marketing, temporarily complicated
by the idea that on account of the war it was the
farmer's duty to forget everything else and produce
to the utmost, regardless of price.

As Weaver entered the ballroom, followed by Cordelia and Dreadwind, the national association of grain
growers in annual convention assembled was singing
a sacred hymn. A large white badge with a man
pinned to it asked Weaver for his ticket of admission.
He shook his head and walked toward the platform
with his hat on. Many faces regarded him curiously.
Before he had reached the platform prayer was announced. He waited in the aisle, still with hat on.
When the prayer was finished he mounted the platform
by the steps at the end and moved toward the front
center, facing the audience. The presiding officer, who
was on the point of introducing the first speaker,
frowned in perplexity and looked about him as if expecting someone to explain away this apparition. No
one offered to do so; and he made a weak intercepting
gesture. But Weaver had already passed him and
was at the front of the platform.

"Some of you know me," he said. "I am Absalom Weaver."

A cheer broke forth. Those who did not know him knew what he was. A wheat-pit gambler on the farmer's side is a crossroad's hero. More than that, he is an inverted sign, a contradiction, an angel of darkness fallen upward. News of him travels weirdly. There was hardly a farmer in the country who by this time had not heard or read some legend of him. Out of the cheering his name was lifted up. Words of rude praise and encouragement were howled at him. The presiding officer shrugged his shoulders and sat down.

Weaver laid his hand on the tumult. Instantly it ceased. His manner chilled them. The notion that he had come to show himself and make a speech was succeeded by a sense of original tragedy transacting. And it was a little unreal, as natural drama is, without setting or perspective. He was seen to be touched with that madness which belongs to prophets. It makes people uneasy. It must be staged or have a painted history; then it is real.

Dreadwind's description of the scene at this moment may have overemphasized its dramatic value. That was as he saw and felt it. To him it was real in all dimensions. Weaver, by an act of rhetorical suspense, by simply holding one cold gesture beyond all expectation, to which you add the strange effect of that unseeing expression peculiar to morbid long-sightedness, stretched his audience to almost the point of groaning. A voice—it might have been that of man or woman— cried hysterically: "What is it?"

Then he spoke in a low penetrating tone.

"Wheat," he said, "is ten dollars a bushel."

The tension snapped; the audible reaction was a stupid titter. That was natural enough. No one knew what he meant. It was possibly a verbal hoax. And some relief from the suspense was a reflex necessity. But it moved Weaver to anger.

"Laugh!" he said. "Laugh. You have learned nothing since you were called dust feet two thousand years ago in Greece. Wheat is ten dollars a bushel. I come to tell you this—to tell you I, Absalom Weaver, in the market place this morning offered that price for all the May wheat in the world and there was none to sell me a peck of it—to tell you I am banished from the pit for having done this, that the pit is closed to both buyers and sellers because the price is beyond the control of your enemies—and you laugh! Simple dust feet! Docile dust feet! Do you know what I am talking about? Do you care? What is it you know? The speculator who sells your wheat before it is grown —do you know what he sells? He sells your labor. Do you know how he sells it? He sells it at auction. A few hundred speculators sell the labor of three million farmers—*at auction!* Do you understand? The pharaohs buying and selling slaves did nothing more. All you want of a slave is his labor. Only now it is a little disguised. Therefore, silly dust feet, you do not see it. They pretend to auction off your wheat, not your labor, and this idle distinction deceives you; but it is the same thing. You do not see it."

He paused and focused his eyes at them. Voices,

not many, called: "Aye, aye. We see it. . . . Yes.
. . . Go on."

"Do you buy the labor of others at auction?"
Weaver continued. "A plow is labor, as a bushel of
wheat is labor. When you buy a plow do you buy it at
auction? Or do you say, when you buy a plow, 'What
will you take for it?' The price of the plow is fixed by
those who have learned to sell their own labor. They
tell you this is necessary. They tell you it is necessary
to fix the price of everything you buy and then to auction off your labor, the sweat of your face, for what
it will bring—and you believe them.

"Why do they sell your produce at auction? Why
do a few hundred speculators thus appoint themselves
to sell your labor? Why, for gain. There is no
other reason. They sell your wheat before you sow it.
They sell it while you tend it. Then when you reap it
they say to you, 'There is too much wheat. There is
a surplus. You have made more breadstuff than people want.' And with saying this they beat you down
until you give up your wheat at a price below that at
which they have already sold it. And you believe them
when they say this is necessary."

Voices: "No! No! We don't believe it. It isn't
so."

"You do," said Weaver. "You may not know it, but
you do. The chains of bondage are imaginary. What
holds the bondsman is his fear. You are afraid. If in
one instant you could overthrow the auction and destroy those who all these years have been selling away
your labor, would you dare? You would be afraid.

They are about to be self-destroyed. The Lord hath
set them in your hand. Did you know it? I find you
singing songs of deliverance. I find you praying.
They neither sing nor pray. To save themselves they
close the auction, shut up the wheat pit which they
have made you believe was an economic necessity,
calling it now a patriotic duty to do so, and here ye sit
by the rivers of Babylon twanging the harp of despair.
When they are saved they will open the pit again.
They are not afraid. I tell you all this and ye laugh."

Directly in front of Weaver a gaunt man rose up.
He was made in Weaver's image, had somewhat of his
manner, and spoke in a strong voice without effort.

"We did not laugh," he said. "Not at that. Say
no more about it. You tell us many things we know.
Tell us something we don't know. What shall we do
with our surplus wheat? How shall we dispose of it?
Tell us that."

"And you say you do not believe them," said
Weaver, full of scorn. "What shall you do with our
surplus? You ask me that and still say you do not believe them. Hear me! There is no surplus. There
never was a surplus. Where is it if there ever was? I
have held in my hands some grains of wheat as old as
the pyramids. If ground into meal they would still
make excellent bread. Wheat is imperishable. Since
the beginning of civilization man has been producing it
diligently. Why have we no store of it? All that man
has been able to produce of it in thousands of years
has been eaten up, saving only seed for the next crop.
Never since Abraham came out of Ur to farm in the

land of Shinar would there have been, if one crop
failed, more than six and a half bushels between man
and starvation. And you talk of a surplus! There is
only the idea of a surplus. The idea of it is the invisible chain that binds you to the auction. It is the fear
with which they have clothed your neck. It is the
mythical stone they have condemned you to roll uphill
forever. There is no surplus. Yet you are continually
running from it, competing with one another to deliver
yourselves into the hands of the auctioneers lest one
shall come last with a bushel of wheat that cannot be
sold at all. And there is no surplus. The utmost there
can ever be is a little wheat over from a fat year to lie
against the want of a lean year. You call this a
surplus?"

The gaunt man rose again. "What shall we do with
that," he asked, "that little over from the fat year?
For we see that in the fat years we are worse off than
ever, the little wheat that shall be over uneaten making
a low price for all that is eaten."

"Keep it," said Weaver. "Keep what is over until
the world's belly swells with hunger. Then it will pay.
Joseph kept grain seven years in a mud storehouse. It
does not spoil. I know what you will say. You will
say you cannot keep it. You have borrowed money at
the bank. You are called upon to pay it back. Therefore you must sell that bushel which breaks the price
of the whole crop. They are demanding it in the market place. I say, do not grow that Satan's bushel. See
to it. But if it be you have grown it, or your neighbor
hath produced it, and they plow your backs too hard

to make you give it up against yourselves at the auction
. . . if you cannot keep it"—here he paused to shape
his period—"then kill it, and the Lord forgive you."

At this confused and contending murmurs rose.
Then voices began to ask: "What of the war?"

His answer was: "They who sell the phantom wheat,
who conjure up a non-existing surplus, who say the price
freely made at auction is what produces wheat, and
now suddenly deny this, now stop the price and shut the
pit to save themselves and name it patriotism—I say,
let them feed the war. Be not deceived. This war of
yours is the oldest war there is."

He probably did not mean in any case to go on.
His thought must have culminated in that apostrophe
to the power of forgiveness. And this at the same
time was his own cry, his own defence. Dreadwind
was the only person present who could have so understood it. Kill the surplus! Kill it, as he had done, and
the Lord forgive them all!

Until then his audience had been in a state of vague
perplexity, inclined as a whole to be sympathetic, yet
with its emotions divided in disorder. But suddenly
he had gone too far. A change took place when the
question was asked: "What about the war?" That
touched a dangerous basic feeling. His answer grossly
offended it. Instantly, therefore, it crystallized against
him. His theme was swept away. In a far corner of
the room a tiny, timorous hiss was heard. Then a
loud one. With no more warning than that the audience raised itself as one many-headed adder and bur-
ried him in hisses, imprecations breaking through.

One would think he must have known; that he had been deliberately heedless. But he was amazed and looked about him in a stricken manner, unable to comprehend it.

Cordelia was running up the aisle. She reached him just as he turned away with a weary sign of defeat. As far as the steps down from the platform he was all right. It was well that Dreadwind met them there, however, for the old man began to lurch. They supported him out and he did not decline their strength. He leaned heavily upon them, whispering: "Quickly, quickly!"

Here Dreadwind omitted the harrowing details. How they got him home he did not say. After having been silent several minutes he skipped all that and began again with what happened next day:

About two o'clock he was sitting with Cordelia in the kitchen. One hates to pass that simple statement. I can see what they were doing. They were at the table, leaning on it. Her hands were lying in his and her eyes were wide and dry. They had not spoken a word for some time. What were they thinking? Nothing. That would be true of the man, I am sure. He was probably tracing the pattern on the oilcloth, over and over, and a tune he had not remembered for years was running around in his head. Water was dripping in the black iron sink. A three-color poster lady in tights was looking down at them from the wall with an eye of skeptical wonder. It was very still.

So Dreadwind was sitting with Cordelia in the kitchen. There was a heavy knock at the door. He went to see; and was not astonished when he stood facing two men in uniform. One was a captain, the other a lieutenant, both new to this business. The captain spoke.

"Is Absalom Weaver here?"

"What is wanted of him?" Dreadwind asked.

"He is wanted."

"By whom?"

The captain hesitated. "We are from the Military Intelligence Bureau," he said.

This Dreadwind had already guessed. And he construed the rest. A man who had publicly proposed to the wheat growers that they should limit their output and destroy their surplus in time of war, with the Government exhorting them to produce more and more, was certain to be charged with disloyalty. It was possible, besides, that the crime of casting rust upon the wheat had at last been traced to him.

"This is where he lived, but he is not here," said Dreadwind.

"We followed him here yesterday from the La Salle Hotel," said the captain. "We have watched ever since. He has not been seen going out."

"No. You wouldn't have seen him go out," said Dreadwind. "But he is not here."

The captain glanced down the hallway. Several men in uniform were at the head of the stairs. "Shall we have to search the place?" he asked.

"That isn't necessary," said Dreadwind. "I'll show you."

He led the two officers down the hall to the door of

Weaver's room, opened it, and stood a little aside.
The officers came on the threshold and looked—at a
long horizontal figure covered with a sheet. The captain went in. He turned down the sheet to uncover
the face, put it back, and came out, his polished military
boots with their silly spurs making a fatuous inept
sound on the bare floor.

"Case closed," he said, and abruptly departed with
his men, whistling on a dry breath.

Thus ended the earthly phase of Absalom Weaver.
Now the other begins. And whether the other was
real in itself or existed fantastically in the minds of
two human beings is a question I wish to leave as I
found it. I have my own reluctant opinion; it is ir-
relevant. I cannot say for certain what Dreadwind's
opinion was. Sometimes I thought he believed it;
then again I thought he didn't. No. He must have
believed it really. At every crucial point the faith of it
lay in his conduct. It does not matter what he thought.

The old man's faculties appear to have been clear
to the end. I mean to say, clear so far as they could
be, bent as they were to his fanatical purpose. First,
he legally authorized Dreadwind to gather up his as-
sets—that is to say his profits in the wheat market; and
then he gave simple, explicit directions as to what
should be done with the money.

"As far as it will go," he said, "do with it as Joseph
did in Egypt. In time of plenty he bought grain. Do
you remember? He gathered grain as the sands of the
sea. Stretch the money. Each year until it is lost buy
wheat in the first glut of the harvest, the new wheat,

in the months of July and September, as the farmers
bring it wet to the auction and dump it."

*   *   *

"Say that again," said Moberly, breaking in.

"In the pit," I said, "what you call July wheat is
the first of the fall-sown crop. September wheat is
the first of the spring-sown crop. Those are the two
new wheat months in the pit. Three-quarters of the
total wheat crop is rushed to market during the harvest
period and sold for what it will bring as July or September wheat. It is the grower's folly. There is a
glut of wheat at this time. Everything overflows and
the price is depressed."

"Yes, yes," said Moberly irritably. "We know all
that. What did he mean about Joseph? That's what
I'm asking. Joseph made a corner in grain, didn't he?
Isn't that what he did?"

"You Board of Trade people say it," I answered.
"Look at Joseph, you say. He was the first great
grain speculator. He saved Egypt. So it was then;
so it is now. Grain speculation is historically necessary. Well, maybe so. I wonder. The fact is that
Joseph did a thing you never heard of one doing on the
Board of Trade. If you heard of one doing it you
would call in his credit and send for his heirs to have
him examined in lunacy."

"What is that?" Moberly asked.

"Joseph bought grain when there was too much of
it, because there was too much of it. Then he sold

it when there was famine. What does the modern grain speculator do when he thinks there is too much wheat? He sells it. What does he do when he thinks there isn't enough? He buys it."

"Rot," said Moberly. "It works out."

"It wouldn't have worked in Egypt," I said. "If there had been a Board of Trade and no Joseph in Egypt what would have happened? During the seven fat years the price of wheat would have been so low, with all the speculators selling it because there was too much, that people would have had to stop growing it. Then when the seven lean years came the quotation for wheat on the Board of Trade might have been a thousand dollars a bushel because there wasn't any and Egypt had perished."

"Stop quarreling," said Goran. "Who cares what Joseph did? Nobody knows. What happened to your precious lovers? I want to know that."

*   *   *

There would be two versions of what Weaver's death did to the lovers. One I can give. That is Dreadwind's. The other—well, a woman never tells. You cannot be sure she could if she would or that she knows. She seems to have no verbal curiosity about her soul's experience.

For Cordelia, whose life hitherto had been dedicated wholly to daughterhood, turning from the father of her being to embrace the miraculous stranger must have been a tremendous emotional act. Perhaps she had not achieved it perfectly and was keeping fire on two altars. There is the other possibility that she had overachieved it and was touched with remorse at not having waited when the end was so near. Or you may believe that the power of the father to command her spirit was even greater in death than it was in life.

What Dreadwind said very simply was that the part of her that was Weaver's seemed to go with him. He said it with a kind of wonder and not at all as if he wished it otherwise. What he did not say, though I knew it to be true, was that the part of her that survived for him was less than he had before. It was and it was not. How shall it be said? She was changed. Her spirit was absent. She had but one compelling thought, which was to act on a revelation that occurred to her as Weaver's life departed. This was irrational. Yet to all circumstances of reality she reacted passively in a rational way notwithstanding; and with Dreadwind she was both infinitely distant and exquisitely near, like someone you love asleep in your arms and dreaming.

Everything else now turns upon that revelation.

After having imparted to Dreadwind very clearly those extraordinary instructions as to how the money should be lost, Weaver said a weird thing. With the ebb of his strength he said that until the money was lost in the way he directed, all of it to the last dollar, his spirit could not leave the earth. It would abide here in suspense. It would dwell in a place he seemed to see and evidently meant to describe; the end was sudden and he failed to get it out.

But Cordelia saw it. She was holding his hand. He was already dead. They were standing at opposite sides of the bed — Dreadwind and Cordelia. She started, her brows contracted violently, and she closed her eyes. When she opened them again they were very wide, her eyebrows were lifted, and she was looking far away.

"A tree!" she whispered.

"Where is it?" Dreadwind asked.

"A tree!" she said again. "What a strange tree!"

"Where?" asked Dreadwind anxiously, for it seemed to him very important to know.

His voice disturbed her. She closed her eyes again, then looked at him with a bothered expression.

"I don't know," she said slowly, remembering his question.

The thought that instantly obsessed her was to find the tree. It was more than a thought. It had the force of a psychic compulsion. Dreadwind could imagine that if she had been alone she would have gone immediately forth into the wide world with that image in her eyes. Almost he could believe that alone, walking in a trance over the face of the earth, she would have found it some time.

But she was not alone. Her anxiety included him so implicitly that they never once spoke of it in question. It was not that she should go to the tree; it was that they should go and be with it, that the three of them should dwell together again in that other place to be discovered. How she should have known, if she did know, that it would be possible for Dreadwind to do this and at the same time carry out Weaver's instructions, is immaterial. It was possible; and it may never have occurred to her to ask whether it was or not.

But there were certain frustrating facts. Dreadwind laid them before her.

First, was the fact that with the whole civilized world in a state of war it was not feasible for people to move about freely on an errand that could not be explained—and the tree, which she described minutely, was clearly a foreign tree. They would have to find it in a strange land.

Secondly, while the war continued it would not be possible to carry out Weaver's instructions in the wheat market, for already the Government was taking steps to fix the price of wheat, thereby suspending speculation altogether.

Thirdly, there was something else. He wondered if she would understand. There was a certain thing men had to do in their own way, without women. It would be necessary on this account for him to leave her. It would not take long; but it was very pressing.

She did understand; at least she accepted his reasons gravely and without comment.

But when he said, therefore, they would be married at once and that she should take his apartment for her own and wait for him there where nothing could touch her, she listened with a tense, thoughtful expression and shook her head.

"Here," she said. "I shall wait here. Wait for him as for the rain," she added musingly.

"But we will be married at once," he said.

Again she shook her head.

"I do not know what marriage is," she said. "I only know that when we are married it shall be all of me."

He protested, argued, insisted. He would marry the tiniest fragment of her, the shadow, the memory and thought of her, and be satisfied. He represented it in a practical light, a romantic light, in the light of his need. She was pleased. He could see in her eyes that she was coming nearer, slowly nearer, as with a great effort of longing, but all the time she kept shaking her head. Then suddenly he lost her. She was snatched back.

"Would it were all of me now," she said. Saying it she dropped her head on her arms and wept bitterly. When he would have touched her consolingly she gently repulsed him.

Thus the father prevailed in spite of them.

CHAPTER XI

WEAVER'S affairs were easy to settle. His estate consisted entirely in credit balances with Board of Trade members; and when the money was all gathered up and put in bank it amounted to nearly a million dollars. Dreadwind was surprised. He had no idea the salvage would be so large.

Then he bade Cordelia good-bye.

She took from around her neck a thin silver chain of very old workmanship, with a locket attached, and put it over his head, dropping the locket inside his collar.

"Bring it back to me unopened," she said.

She stood with her back to the kitchen table, her hands grasping the edges of it, her body inclined a little toward him.

"You will find me here like this. I shall hear you coming. The door will not be locked. Open it without knocking. You will think I had never stirred."

What he did in the war I don't know. I think it was the tank corps. Hating publicity, he enlisted by an assumed name, or I should have looked it up. He merely said he went in at a place where he could count on a prompt discharge when the show was over. Anyhow, he returned with a slight limp.

When he opened the door, with a sudden panic and faintness of heart, there she stood, exactly as he had seen her last, only a little more inclined toward him,

192

her lips parted, a high light in her eyes. She was wholly present at that moment. Her spirit was there and touched him. She looked him once over with swift anxiety and threw her arms about his neck, at the same time exploring him for the silver locket which, when it was found, she took back.

His ecstasy in that phase was brief. Almost at once she changed again, her eyes once more had that look of far-seeing, and there was an air of impatience about her.

Now, two things remained to be done in order that a third might happen. The first thing was to arrange that Weaver's money should be lost in the wheat pit, agreeably to his instructions. The next was to find the tree in which his spirit was supposed to be lingering Then it was only to abide the sequel.

There was a broker on the Board of Trade whom Dreadwind trusted as he would trust himself—even more. I do not know his name. He appears to have been a man in whose house gambling in wheat was neither prohibited nor encouraged. It took its place. His true interest lay rather in the handling of actual grain as a dealer. He was an ideal broker for the purpose, since no one would expect him to be handling an irrational gambling account in the phantom stuff of the pit, and his business in actual grain was more than large enough to conceal the other. Dreadwind went to this broker and gave him the strangest order that was ever placed on the Board of Trade. It was an order, you understand, to lose a million dollars in the pit. Only of course it was not said that way. Specifically, it was an order to buy July and September wheat in the pit, on the glut of the harvest, at the highest prices possible, until the money was all gone. When it was lost then the account was to close and Dreadwind was to be notified. The broker stared at him stupidly.

"I know," said Dreadwind. "It's perfectly mad. I can't explain it and I can't be here to do it myself. That's why I bring it to you. Imagine it to be an affair of the conscience and let it go at that."

"Pity to wallow that kind of conscience around in the wheat pit," said the broker. However, he accepted the commission, and that was that. They thought it was. No one had the faintest doubt as to what would happen to the money. Weaver hadn't; Dreadwind hadn't; the broker hadn't.

Well, now Cordelia and Dreadwind set out together. All they had to go on was her description of the tree. She had never seen one like it. Neither had Dreadwind. Yet neither of them doubted its existence; and Cordelia was sure she would know it at sight. She led the way. I mean it was her impulse always that guided them. And when at length they had found that kind of tree they were no nearer than when they started; for of the teak species there are millions scattered through the forests of Asia. Fancy the chance of finding one! Of finding a certain one with not the slightest physical notion of where it was! It seems often true in human experience that the sense of probability is suspended. Something else goes on working in its place. We cannot imagine what that is. There are those who prefer the supernatural explanation, which leaves it as it was. Others say there is a vast region of the human mind yet to be explored. It has faculties both vestigal and rudimentary which we use unawares. That may be so.

There were times when Cordelia lost all sense of direction and then they drifted in an aimless way, merely looking. Then by one impulse they would go a month's journey in a straight line, looking neither right nor left, only to be disappointed again at the end. And yet a chart of their movements—Dreadwind had plotted one and showed it to me—clearly revealed a blind tendency from every angle to converge upon a certain point.

For some time Dreadwind had been silent, smoking slowly, his thoughts dwelling upon their travels, as I knew from now and then a wistful smile upon his face or an involuntary contraction of the grief muscles in his forehead.

"That's all," he said suddenly. "You passed us several times, you say. Therefore you know. It took us nearly three years to find it."

"How long?" I asked.

"Nearly three years."

"Then it wasn't true?"

"What wasn't true?"

"Weaver's notion about his spirit. Three years, you say. Well? His spirit ought long ago to have departed. And if it had, or you thought it had, you would not continue here."

"Oh! I see," he said, his puzzled look breaking

away. "You assume that the money has been lost. Of course. Anyone would think so. I haven't told you. It sounds incredible. The money has not been lost. On the contrary, it has multiplied. I could show you the broker's reports. The first year half of it was lost. The next year the surviving half increased itself threefold. And this year—I've just heard—it has doubled. It now amounts to about three million dollars."

"And the tree meanwhile is flourishing," I commented.

He looked at me steadily, nodding his head. "I don't suppose anyone ever tried to lose money in the wheat pit," he said. "It may be in the nature of chance that it's as hard to lose as to win if that's what you set out to do. Of course . . . I might . . . No, I couldn't do that. We shall have to see."

What it was he might do he did not say and I did not ask. One is permitted to guess.

It was strange that Weaver's money had not been lost. But you see, in placing it Dreadwind had in mind not the losing of it primarily but the effect Weaver wished it to have in the pit, which was to support the price of wheat in the glut of the harvest; and it had been demonstrated to everyone's amazement that money employed in that way need not be lost. It was the Joseph thing over again—buying grain when there was too much of it because there was too much, and, behold! it turned out to pay. Yes, but on the other side, if Dreadwind now wished more to lose the money than to prove Weaver's theory he could very easily do so. Any experienced wheat gambler would know how to do that. Superstition aside, one could do it with certainty.

Dreadwind's dilemma is clear. He was torn between an impulse to break the spell that enthralled them both and a powerful sentiment of veneration for the form and meaning of it. I have said once that I could not be sure that in his mind he believed it at all, and that yet he unconsciously did, for believing was implicit in his acts. Here it was. He would not change those first instructions to the broker in any way to place the money in greater jeopardy.

There he is. I leave him to you. A man living in a bamboo hut with the woman he loves and cannot possess, unable to destroy the invisible thing that keeps them apart.

CHAPTER XII

"A NIGHT'S tale," I said, looking around the table. "Dawn is breaking. So it was in Burma when Dreadwind finished."

Sylvester and Selkirk looked first at the sky over the sea and then at their watches. Goran stretched. Moberly sat quite still. He was the first to speak.

"How long ago was that?" he asked. "When were you with Dreadwind, I mean?"

"Four months ago," I said. "A little more. Four and a half."

"They are there still?" he asked.

"Yes," I said.

"Waiting for old Weaver's money to be lost?"

"Yes."

I noticed that he framed these questions carefully and I wondered, too, at their sincerity. I had not expected him to be the one most impressed.

Chairs were pushed back.

"Wait a minute," said Goran. "I've a feeling you have left something out. Something about Cordelia. Didn't you see her before you left?"

"Yes."

"Alone?"

I hesitated for an answer and marveled at Goran's subtle penetration.

"You did of course," he said, not waiting. "And

I have a feeling that she spoke with you to some purpose. That is what is missing."

"I suspect you know too much about women," I said.

"Only that they are unknowable," he answered. "Can you tell us what she said?"

This was what she said. Goran apparently had already guessed it, not the words, but the sense. She had been with us for breakfast. It was nine o'clock when we were ready to start for the boat landing. She meant to go with us, and we were on the veranda waiting for Dreadwind. He called out that he would overtake us; he had a letter to finish that he wished me to post. So we walked on through the forest without him—Cordelia and I. As we passed the tree I noticed she did not look at it; and her not doing so was rather pointed, since she must have been aware that I was regarding it with deep curiosity.

"The day will be very hot," she said. "I'm sorry to have kept you up all night. Mr. Dreadwind told you, did he not, it was I who wished you to know everything?"

"Yes," I answered, "he told me that. And he seemed a little surprised," I added.

She ignored the provocative part of my statement and was silent for several minutes.

"Are you familiar with the wheat pit?" she asked.

I said that I was.

"Is it so difficult to lose money there if that is one's real intention?" she asked. As I did not reply at once she added: "You know what I mean."

"I know what you mean," I said. "No, I shouldn't have thought it would be so difficult. But it's hard to say. There is no experience, you see. Never before has anyone tried to lose money there."

That was as far as I was willing at the time to satisfy Goran's curiosity. There was more. And there was the sign. I did not tell him of that either. He was regarding me with a superior indulgent smile; and when he understood that I meant to tell no more he said: "Enough. Men are so stupid! They don't deserve their luck, now do they? We never know what we want. Only the woman does."

What else passed there on the forest path before Dreadwind overtook us is no longer inhibited, and may as well be set down at once. My reply as to the difficulty of losing money in the wheat pit left her dissatisfied, though she did not say so. She said nothing. After a little while I said: "Why did you so particularly wish me to know?" She did not answer, therefore I added: "I ask because I haven't been told how I shall treat it. I mean, whether to treat it as if I had never heard it . . . or——" I stopped, hardly knowing myself what I wished to say. I had only the intuition that somewhere in all this lay a veiled purpose; also the feeling that I was expected to sense it. And the assumption that I am a subtle person causes me always a little irritation, precisely because I am not.

"You are going back," she said.

"Yes," I said. "Directly back."

It was then, as I said in the beginning, that she drew me a little aside. We had come to the landing and Dreadwind was not yet in sight. She stood with her hands behind her, the sun in her face, her eyes wide open; and I saw for myself the expression that had so long baffled Dreadwind. When she spoke she was not as before. She was not quite herself. Her words were stilted. "In a far place," she said, "by the water, you will be alone among many people. Four men will meet you as if by chance. They will take you to sup with them. Tell them, and tell no one else until then. Only be sure they are the right men. You will think of a sign."

Then Dreadwind came with his letter and bade me good-bye.

None of this did I tell at the table.

We broke up. The others were for going to bed and spoke of meeting at lunch time; but Sylvester asked me to go for a walk. I went. We had taken a long turn down the boardwalk and were watching the sun rise out of the sea when he said, most abruptly:

"I am that broker."

"What broker?" I asked, unable for an instant to make any connection of ideas.

"The one that has old Weaver's money under Dreadwind's instructions," he said. "I thought all the time it was Dreadwind's own. He told me only what he appears to have repeated to you—that he couldn't explain it and I might regard it as an affair of conscience. All of that Weaver stuff was new to me."

"How extraordinary!" I exclaimed.

"But what on earth prompted you to tell the story in that company?" he asked. His tone was disapproving.

"I was prompted. That's all I can say," I answered.

"Well, you've done it all right," he said.

"What do you mean?"

"I mean you've turned the cards face up. That's the end of Weaver's money."

"I begin to see," I said; "but go on."

"Didn't you notice a change in Moberly's face toward the end."

"If I did," I said, "I failed to construe it. What was it?"

"You might not have noticed it," he said. "You were telling the story. Everyone else did."

"But what was it?"

"It was that look any hunting animal has, man or beast, when the image of prey falls suddenly upon the eye. Look. Weaver's three million dollars in the wheat pit. You have told Moberly the money is there. You have told him how it is played in July and September wheat—not only how it has been played but how it will continue to be played until it is lost. You have shown him all the cards. Now you see. He will get it. He will not rest until he does."

"May you be right," I said; which surprised him, for that was not his state of feeling. I understood what his reaction was. He had none of Goran's sentimental insight. He was deeply shocked by the fact that a matter left secretly to his care and responsibility in terms of unlimited trust had been rudely exposed. Now he was helpless. The Weaver-Dreadwind account would be slaughtered in his hands and he could not save it. A broker would feel that way; a broker like Sylvester would.

"And Goran was right," I answered. "A woman knows what she wants."

That was too much. He regarded me with gloomy disfavor not at all concealed, and so we parted.

I did not see them again—not then. They went their way and I went mine. When I thought of it I devoutly wished that Sylvester's foreboding should not be disappointed; also that he would be unable to communicate with Dreadwind, who might be tempted to protect the money. I learned afterward that he had tried to get word to Dreadwind, but it was too late.

The next August it occurred that I was passing through Chicago and the impulse came to me suddenly to stop and call on Sylvester. How easily one puts aside what is not one's own. I at least am that kind of person. Although Dreadwind's affair interested me enormously I had not thought of it for several weeks. I might have been half around the world before thinking of it again. And here I was, in the city of the wheat pit, where the sequel would be, if one there was.

Sylvester was too busy to see anyone, they told me at his office door; it was with much difficulty that I got my name to him. He sent out for me immediately.

I found him standing at the grain ticker in his private office. He looked at me as I came in and turned his eyes again to the tape. I stood for several minutes at his side, looking at it too. September wheat was 94½ and the quotations were coming fast.

"Rather active," I said.

"Rather," he replied, dryly.

The price was falling: 94⅜ . . . 94¼ . . . 94⅛

. . . then back to 94¼. I could imagine what was going on in the wheat pit—how wild and excited it was, how savage the uproar. In Sylvester's office, however, there was no sound but the steady purr and gnash of the ticker.

"And the sellers seem to have it," I said.

"Don't you know what is happening?" he asked. "You ought to be interested. Moberly is shooting for Weaver's money. He's got the hide. There's only a little of the tail left and he wants that too. See!" He crimped the tape at the last quotation for September wheat, which was 94⅛. "When the price touches 94, as it will, that will be tail and all. There!"

The very next quotation was 94. He flung the tape down and turned away.

"Well," he said, facing me suddenly. "How do you like it?"

"I am delighted," I said. "And don't let it run in your head that I was a blundering idiot who brought a tale to the wrong place."

Then to comfort him I told him why. He listened with a neutral air and at the end he grunted.

Two months passed. I took no steps to satisfy my curiosity, for by this time I had placed the Dreadwind romance in a field by itself, an irrational field, where the bit of superstition which survives in the most unbelieving of us might have its orgy out. The end would disclose itself, I said, in its own way. And so it did.

One evening in a London hotel, while I was dressing, a note was brought in. Compliments of Mr. and Mrs.

Dreadwind, and would I be pleased to dine with them in their rooms? They were in the same hotel.

They greeted me as if I had rights in them—as shy children bursting with a secret that you must not suspect the existence of but stumble upon amazedly in the dark. It was no secret. Anyhow, it cannot be told. All the words about it are silly. You have to see it. I could hardly see anything else. And it was something a lone, selfish man ought not to be permitted to see. For his own sake he ought not to see it. It makes his world seem very empty for a while and it is never quite the same again, even when he thinks he has got well over it.

They pressed me with food and wordless attentions and laughed together at the little mishaps that came of their anxiety to include me in their happiness; which of course made me feel as one who sitteth outside the wall in gross darkness and hath no way of communion. They did speak of their plans. They were going to Kansas to buy a farm—a certain farm, one they had fastened their hearts upon—and make them a paradise.

"A large farm?" I asked. "Tell me about it?"

They were a little embarrassed and then smiled together. Of course. They knew nothing about this farm except that in the front yard was an apple tree with a bench around it, and that across and down the road was a wheat field where a mystical experience had befallen them one morning in the dawn.

When I had made sure there were no untouchable recollections I said: "I was with Sylvester the day the last of the money was lost," and I was going on to describe the scene when suddenly a look of extreme surprise appeared on Dreadwind's face. Cordelia was gazing at me pensively. I turned it off abruptly. There was a silence.

"Then you knew Sylvester?" Dreadwind asked.

"Very well," I said.

"But I never told you he was the broker."

That was a tight place for me. It was clear that Cordelia and I knew more than Dreadwind. She was still gazing at me, more with wondering what I should say than with any sign of uneasiness.

"No, you didn't," I said. "But you will recall that as you were telling me the story out there in the bamboo hut and came to the fact of the money having multiplied itself incredibly you spoke of showing me the broker's reports, as though I might look at them if I cared to do so. Well, some of them were lying there open on the table. Naturally I glanced at them, and I couldn't very well help seeing the broker's name in large type at the top of every sheet."

That passed. Cordelia smiled, not as one smiles whose anxiety is happily relieved but as if she were amused.

"What I meant to ask," I said, "was how you knew when the end came?"

"We knew it at once," said Dreadwind. "The same day."

"How?"

"By the shadow," he said simply. Then he added: "Sylvester sent a cable message, but it missed us on our way out. I first heard from him here in London only two weeks ago."

They bought the farm in Kansas. I have seen them there many times. I hate to go because of what happens to my own world when I see them together; and yet I cannot resist it.

Only a few days ago I met Goran again.

"Have you found out yet what was in that silver locket?" he asked. He meant the locket Cordelia gave to Dreadwind when he went to war, with instructions to bring it back unopened. Goran had already asked me this question three times.

"Wheat," I said. "Two grains of wheat."

"Don't try to be stupid," he said. "What two grains of wheat? I have guessed, but I want to know for sure."

I told him.

Cordelia went back and got two grains of ripe wheat from the very stalk at which she, Dreadwind and Weaver knelt down in the dawn to witness one of Nature's most beautiful acts. They were in the locket. And they were planted on the Dreadwind farm. I have myself eaten bread from them. It is served on wedding anniversaries.

THE END

9 781610 160896